8/1 $ 3⁹⁵

Learning Disabilities

LEARNING
DISABILITIES

James J. McCarthy

UNIVERSITY OF WISCONSIN

Joan F. McCarthy

Allyn and Bacon, Inc.
Boston

Library of Congress Catalog Card Number: 78-86836

Printed in the United States of America.

Fourth printing . . . April, 1971

CONTENTS

FOREWORD

AT THE TURN OF THE CENTURY, school classes for handicapped children—the mentally retarded, the deaf, the blind, the physically handicapped—were few and far between. Classes or programs for children with severe learning problems were practically nonexistent. Today programs for handicapped children are a part of most school systems. But in spite of the progress made in services for children with recognized handicaps, there remains a sizeable group of children who have severe problems in learning to talk, to think, to perceive and/or who are failing to learn the three R's in school. They do not fit into the traditional categories of handicapped children, and yet they are handicapped since they are unable to develop normally in all phases of growth.

This group of children (whose problems are now labeled "learning disabilities") is not an homogenous group. It includes children with various psychological and educational developmental deficits but who are normal in sensory, physical, or intellectual attributes. They have been variously labeled, depending not only on their type of difficulty but also on the professional discipline that makes the diagnosis. A physician might diagnose a child as dyslexic, while an educator might label him as a severe case of reading disability. A neurologist might label a child as brain damaged; a psychiatrist might label him as emotionally disturbed; and a psychologist might say his trouble stems from poor visual perception.

Because of the wide variety of disabilities found under the umbrella of "learning disabilities" a plethora of books and articles has appeared, each describing one or several of the disabilities found. Very often they describe small segments of the broader problem, or view the difficulties from the narrow perspective of a particular theory or a particular practice. Reading these diverse books and articles, one becomes confused about the real problems encountered by children with learning disabilities. It appears at times like the three blind men who had been asked to describe an elephant. One felt the leg and described the elephant as a trunk of a tree. Another felt the side and described the elephant as a side of a barn, while the third, feeling the tail, described the elephant as a rope. Each was aware of one valid part of the whole, while none could describe the elephant as a whole. Thus some of the divergent literature under the label "learning disabilities" reminds us of the descriptions of an elephant given by the blind men.

The authors have done a unique service in attempting to bring order out of chaos. Unlike others they have no special system or point of view they are advocating. Instead, they have collated the information from a variety of sources and have tried to answer relevant questions raised by students. In doing so they reviewed (a) the historical development of the field, (b) identification and etiology, (c) prevalence, (d) diagnostic procedures, (e) various educational procedures, (f) representative classroom programs, and (g) other related problems. To collate this material from numerous sources, and to differentiate the diagnostic procedures and educational methods required a great deal of selectivity and perspective.

Although the authors modestly state in the Preface "We do not think it is possible to write a distinguished treatise on the subject of learning disabilities at this time. . ." their book belies their modesty for they have probably come as close to interpreting the field as is possible.

Students will find within this book a brief and concise review of the theories and status of "learning disabilities." It presents objectively the consensus and viewpoints of diverse authors, synthesizes the divergent points of view, and describes the major remedial methods advocated. Students will appreciate this clarification of the field as an introduction to the understanding of the vast literature now accumulated in books and journals.

SAMUEL A. KIRK

PROFESSOR
DEPT. OF SPECIAL EDUCATION
UNIVERSITY OF ARIZONA

PREFACE

We do not think it is possible to write a distinguished treatise on the subject of learning disabilities at this time, though many would yearn to write such a book and even more to read it. There is no such thing as professional consensus on the subject because there is so little in the way of firm data to support a given point of view. Yet, in a field where facts are few, fervor runs high. Beliefs are often held with great conviction; facts speak for themselves but beliefs require spokesmen. Professional convictions are by no means whimsical, arbitrary, or self-enhancing, though, unfortunately, many are not compatible. One finds all shades of opinion. For example, some would deny the existence of learning disabilities as an entity while others would seek to distinguish learning "disabilities" from "disorders" on the basis of degree of defect. To some, *learning disabilities* means children with a specific kind of impairment, while to others it is a generic term meaning all those children whose primary problem lies in their incapacity to utilize ordinary school procedures for learning. When experts do not concur on definition, terminology, treatment, and so on, a unified and unbiased viewpoint is not possible.

Clearly, a book is a premature undertaking in this field. Yet pressures for service have catapulted professionals into attempts to teach such children, to train teachers for them, and to write legislation for them. Thus, there will be writings, premature or not. But the authors must be content to present the varied points of view and the readers must be prepared to tolerate ambiguity. Moreover, no author can be completely unbiased. For example, it is clear that in order to discuss the matter of prevalence rates, one must first define what one is counting. Thus, one either tentatively accepts definitions or ignores prevalence. The point to be made here is that some bias cannot be avoided.

Acceptance of the term *learning disabilities* by the professionals in special education represents one of those quiet revolutions that infrequently occur in a field. This term has come to be acknowledged as representing a real entity, a type of child, that can benefit from certain special educational procedures. The virtues of this term, in our judgment, outnumber its drawbacks. It describes the child's school behavior rather than assigning its cause. Terms like *visually handicapped, socially maladjusted,* and *mentally retarded* are etiological in character and tend to diagnose the child's behavior rather than simply describe it. The advantage to descriptive labeling is that educators are trained to deal with observed behavior, not broad etiological categories. These latter tend to have more meaning for the medical profession, where etiology often indicates a course of action.

The term *learning disabilities* is occasioning a reorientation of special educators about all exceptional children. After all, almost all exceptional children could be described, by definition, as having some kind of learning disability. Yet, not all exceptional children can be placed in this category because the methods of teaching to various types of disabilities may vary considerably. The visually impaired, for example, have learning problems, but they do not stem essentially from a disoriented learning apparatus. In time, then, the appearance of the term *learning disabilities* could occasion a restructuring of educational thought which, in turn, would precipitate needed changes in special educational practices and in the in-service and pre-service training of special educators.

For better or worse, the term *learning disabilities* is now part of the legacy bequeathed to budding professionals in the behavioral sciences. So, regardless of the state of the art, it is reasonable to ask questions about children with learning disabilities, such as:

What is a learning disability?

What causes a learning disability?

What are the distinguishing characteristics of children with learning disabilities?

What can be done to nullify the effects of learning disabilities?

This book is an attempt to answer these and other questions in the most useful possible way.

JAMES J. McCARTHY

JOAN F. McCARTHY

ACKNOWLEDGMENTS

FOR THEIR ASSISTANCE IN REVIEWING parts of the manuscript related to their programs, grateful acknowledgment is made to Professor Raymond Barsch of Southern Connecticut Teacher's College; Professor Barbara Bateman of the University of Oregon; Carl Delacato, Ph.D., Associate Director of the Institutes for the Achievement of Human Potential; Kathleen Fitzhugh, Ph.D., Assistant Professor of Psychology, Department of Neurology, Indiana University; Marianne Frostig, Executive Director, Marianne Frostig Center of Educational Therapy; Professor Newell Kephart, Executive Director, Achievement Center for Children, Purdue University; Laura Lehtinen, Ph.D., Clinical Director, The Cove Schools, Racine, Wisconsin and Evanston, Illinois; Mrs. Margaret Rawson, President, The Orton Society, Inc., Mrs. Samuel Orton, Director, The Orton Reading Clinic, Winston-Salem, N.C.; Wayne Otto, Ph.D., Professor, Research in Basic Skills Laboratory, University of Wisconsin; and Douglas Wiseman, Ed.D., St. Paul Public Schools, St. Paul, Minnesota.

We wish to acknowledge the assistance of the following in permitting us to visit their programs and/or for reviewing the resulting portions of manuscript: Jeanne McCarthy, Ph.D., University of Illinois-Chicago and formerly Director, Program of Remediation for Children with Severe Learning Disabilities, and the staff of Schaumburg Community Consolidated School District No. 54, Hoffman Estates, Illinois; Professor Francis Blair, Director, and Mrs. Laura Washa, Teacher-Administrator, Special Learning Disabilities Laboratory, University of Wisconsin-Milwaukee; Professor James Olson, Department of Exceptional Education, University of Wisconsin-Milwaukee; George Stockton, Ph.D., Director of Pupil Services, and Miriam Magdol, teacher S.L.D. Class, Madison Public Schools, Madison, Wisconsin.

Our thanks, also, to: Mrs. Diana Perkins, President of the California Association for Neurologically Handicapped Children for her assistance with the portion of the manuscript dealing with parent groups; to Corrine Kass, Ph.D., University of Arizona and formerly U.S. Office of Education for information on federal programs; John Melcher, Assistant Superintendent of Public Instruction and Chief, Bureau for Handicapped Children, Wisconsin, for his assistance with the manuscript relating to legislation; and Professor Samuel Kirk, University of Arizona, for his helpful commentary on the manuscript.

Finally, we wish to thank Mrs. Dorothy S. Warren for her assistance in typing the manuscript and Mr. David Logan for preparing resource and research listings.

1

BACKGROUND and DEFINITION

of LEARNING DISABILITIES

A LEARNING DISABILITY refers to a retardation, disorder, or delayed development in one or more of the processes of speech, language, reading, writing, arithmetic, or other school subjects resulting from a psychological handicap caused by a possible cerebral dysfunction and/or emotional or behavioral disturbances. It is not the result of mental retardation, sensory deprivation, or cultural or instructional factors.*

Perhaps no other single label connotes a greater variety of seemingly unrelated conditions than the term *learning disabilities.* Conditions classified as learning disabilities include, among others, dyslexia, dysgraphia, perceptual handicap, neurological impairment, and autism. Professional reaction to this diverse assortment has been characterized by Capobianco: "Perhaps the one irrefutable characteristic attributable to children with learning disabilities is their wide variety of behavior."[1]

There is no clear professional unanimity for the meaning of the term *learning disabilities,* although the Kirk[2] definition given above and that of the National Advisory Committee on Handicapped Children given in Chapter 7 probably represent the best available consensus statements.

---

* Samuel A. Kirk and Barbara Bateman, "Diagnosis and Remediation of Learning Disabilities," *Exceptional Children* 29, No. 2 (Oct. 1962): 73.

Perhaps the best way to understand the present status of the concept of learning disabilities is to trace the forces responsible for fashioning that concept.

In 1942, Kurt Goldstein published a report on his observations of brain-injured adults, *Aftereffects of Brain Injuries in War*. Even after brain injuries were physically healed, such persons exhibited a disordered behavior, which could include emotional lability, perceptual disturbances, and distractibility.

These reactions were beyond normal limits—that is, they were out of proportion to the cause. Emotionally labile patients, for example, when confronted with a task beyond their ability to perform, might experience a strong reaction of rage, despair, anxiety, and extreme depression, with all the accompanying body reactions of crying, changing color, trembling, and so on. Goldstein called this reaction the *catastrophic reaction* of a brain-injured organism.

In 1947, A. A. Strauss and Laura Lehtinen published their classic text, *Psychopathology and Education of the Brain-Injured Child*. In their work with mentally retarded children at the Cove Schools, the authors found it useful to distinguish between endogenous and exogenous retardates. These latter, whose retardation was presumably due to an external cause (i.e., brain injury), seemed qualitatively different than the former and exhibited behavior not unlike that of Goldstein's adult subjects. The Strauss and Lehtinen text, a report of their rationale, experiments, and methods, was to have great influence in special education. Exogenous children were described as hyperactive, emotionally labile, perceptually disordered, impulsive, distractible, and perseverative. This collection of symptoms came to be known as the *Strauss Syndrome,* or the *brain-injured* syndrome.

Many children who had school difficulties also exhibited one or more of these symptoms. At the same time, they did not fit into any of the existing etiologic categories (e.g., mental retardation, deafness). The concept of brain-injury seemed applicable in such cases and found rapid acceptance among professional special educators. Doubtless, the rather complete set of methodologies supplied for such children by Strauss and Lehtinen enhanced acceptance of the concept. It is instructive to compare the definition of the *brain-injured child,* proposed by Strauss and Lehtinen,[3] with the definition of *learning disabilities,* proposed by Kirk[4] at the beginning of this chapter. The former defined a brain-injured child as:

> A . . . child who before, during, or after birth has received an injury to or suffered an infection of the brain. As a result of such organic impairment, defects in the neuromotor system may be present or absent; however, such a child may show disturbances in perception, thinking, and emotional behavior, either separately or in combination. These disturbances prevent or impede a normal learning process. Special educational methods have been devised to remedy these specific handicaps.

The rose was not without thorns. Birch[5] stated the problem well:

> Considerable confusion has resulted from the use of this term (brain-injured child), since, from its first application until the present, two problems have persisted: (1) evidence that children exhibiting the behavioral pattern described do in fact have damage to the brain is poor, and (2) many children with known and independently verified brain damage (i.e., non-behavioral neurologic or anatomic evidence) do not exhibit the patterns of behavior presumably characteristic of "brain damage." At the risk of provoking a useless semantic storm, it must be noted that attaching the adjective "minimal" to the term "brain damage" does not increase the descriptive accuracy of the term or add either to its scientific validity or its usefulness. Regardless of any adjectives, we have the over-riding obligation to demonstrate, in terms of replicatable, valid, and clearly defined criteria, that the multiplicity or aberrant behaviors we now attribute to "minimal brain damage" are, in fact, the result of damage to the brain.

The term *learning disabilities* began appearing with regularity in the early 1960's largely as a substitute for *brain-injured*. By referring to behavior, rather than etiology, the term *learning disability* circumvented objections such as Birch's. However, the logical inconsistencies associated with the concept of the brain-injured child were not dissipated by the act of providing it a new name. For example, it is no more logical for emotionally disturbed children to be regarded as learning-disabled than it is for them to be regarded as brain injured, perhaps even less so. Historically, however, many symptoms described by Goldstein and Strauss appeared to be more emotional than intellectual in nature. Hence, emotional problems with a presumptive neurological basis fit Strauss's concept of brain-injured child but at first could appear incongruous if that concept were labeled *learning disability*.

Remedial attempts with children having learning disabilities did not clarify the issue. Even as Strauss emphasized the visual-perceptual approach for remediation (occasioned in no small part by his background in Gestalt psychology), others have emphasized approaches to remediation aimed at different characteristic defects of children with learning disabilities (occasioned in no small part by their backgrounds). One can discern, for example, a linguistic approach (Bateman, 1964), a motoric approach (Kephart, 1960), a movement approach (Barsch, 1965), a neurological reorganization approach (Delacato, 1963), a visual-perceptual approach (Frostig, 1964), the application of tactual techniques (Fernald, 1943), and other approaches not as neatly characterizable (e.g., Getman, 1964; Haeussermann, 1958).

As each of these approaches found expression in the professional literature, there was a tendency for each to define learning disabilities in terms of the particular stress of its own methodology. Thus, learning disabilities are seen by some as basically linguistic and by others as basically motoric, and by still others as basically perceptual. The application of the term *learning disabilities* to many diverse conditions led naturally to the notion that this term might serve as a unifying concept in the field of special education. Clements[6] summarized the problems inherent in this approach, stating:

> Although the . . . viewpoint may represent a much needed philosophical reorientation within the field of special education, it holds little practical promise for the near future since it will involve a de-emphasis of "specialty" areas within special education, and a complete revision of teacher preparation and certification. To my knowledge, although talked about, no teacher training facility is willing, at present, to reorganize its various programs along this line.

He recommended, instead, that the term *learning disabilities* be the educational alternative to the diagnosis of minimal brain dysfunctions, which he defined as:[7]

> . . . Children of near average, average, or above average general intelligence with learning and/or certain behavioral abnormalities ranging from mild to severe, which are associated with subtle deviant function of the central nervous system. These may be char-

acterized by various combinations of deficit in perception, concep-
tualization, language, memory, and control of attention, impulse, or
motor function.

Thus, where intelligence is essentially normal, and in the absence
of valid evidence to the contrary, the behavioral, language, and
school subject deficits noted in Kirk's definition of learning disabilities are seen as symptoms of subtle cerebral dysfunction in school
aged children. Such children are said to have learning disabilities.

Under the circumstances, it is difficult if not impossible to com-
pose an inclusive and universally acceptable definition of learning
disabilities.[8] None the less, historical evidence appears to recommend the Kirk[2] definition. It will, then, be the definition of the
term *learning disabilities* that we use in the remainder of this book.

REFERENCES

1. R. F. CAPOBIANCO, "Diagnostic Methods Used With Learning Disabilities Cases," *Exceptional Children* 31, no. 4 (Dec. 1964): 187.
2. SAMUEL A. KIRK, "The Illinois Test of Psycholinguistic Abilities: Its
   Origin and Implications." In *Learning Disorders,* Vol. 3, Jerome Hellmuth, ed. (Seattle, Washington: Special Child Publications, 1968).
   In this publication, Kirk has modified his definition of learning disability as follows: "A learning disability refers to a specific retardation
   or disorder in one or more of the processes of speech, language perception, behavior, reading, spelling, writing, or arithmetic." This
   definition is more concise since it omits reference to etiology. It adds
   the word "specific" before retardation. In essence, however, the concept remains unchanged. The interested reader will find a rational
   and well-thought-through exposition of the concept of learning
   disabilities in this source.
3. ALFRED A. STRAUSS and LAURA LEHTINEN, *Psychopathology and Education of the Brain Injured Child* (New York: Grune and Stratton,
   1947) p. 4.
4. SAMUEL A. KIRK and BARBARA BATEMAN, "Diagnosis and Remediation of Learning Disabilities," *Exceptional Children* 29, no. 2 (Oct.
   1962): 73.
5. HERBERT G. BIRCH, ed., *Brain Damage in Children* (Baltimore: Williams and Wilkins Co., 1964) pp. 4-5, Courtesy Association for the
   Aid of Crippled Children, New York, N. Y.

6. SAM D. CLEMENTS, "Learning Disabilities—Who?" Abstract published in *Special Education: Strategies for Educational Progress,* Selected Convention Papers, 44th Annual CEC Convention, April 17-24th, 1966a (Washington, D. C.: The Council for Exceptional Children, N.E.A., 1201 Sixteenth St. N.W.) pp. 188-189.
7. CLEMENTS, Abstract in *Special Education: Strategies for Educational Progress,* 44th CEC Convention papers, pp. 188-189.
8. A concise statement characterizing learning disabilities was developed by the National Advisory Committee on Handicapped Children and can be found on p. 34 of their first Annual Report, Jan. 31, 1968. This statement is detailed in Chapter 7.

2

IDENTIFICATION, ETIOLOGY

and EPIDEMIOLOGY

AN EXCEPTIONAL CHILD is one who, because of a clearly identifiable disability, deviates in educationally significant ways to such an extent that he requires special educational procedures. Therefore, a child with a learning disability, as we have defined him, is not necessarily exceptional. Indeed, it is precisely our inability to identify the specific cause of the observed learning deficit that characterizes the child with learning disabilities. Moreover, the overall educational impairment of such a child, as a general rule, requires procedures not available in the normal classroom but is usually not of sufficient magnitude to warrant special class placement. In addition, a learning disability is usually not as generalized as other, more clearly identifiable disabilities. Instead, it is often limited to specific areas of classroom performance and/or certain behavioral manifestations that occur under given circumstances. A child with learning disabilities will have educationally significant deviations *among his own performances.* Such a child seems normal in some ways and deviant in others.

The educator's problems begin with (a) identifying the child with possible learning disabilities in the school population, (b) distinguishing the child with learning disabilities from the child who has learning problems for reasons other than presumed minimal cerebral dysfunction, and (c) determining how many such

7

children he will have to provide for. These problems are considered in the present chapter under the respective headings of identification, etiology and epidemiology.

IDENTIFICATION

Children with learning disabilities come to the attention of the schools for a number of reasons. Perhaps the most exhaustive list of such reasons, which he culled from over one hundred recent publications, was compiled by Clements.[1] Around one hundred specific behaviors were listed under sixteen general headings (e.g., disorders of attention and concentration, disorders of motor function, etc.). However, the ten most frequently cited characteristics of such children, in order of frequency cited, were:

1. Hyperactivity.
2. Perceptual-motor impairments.
3. Emotional lability.
4. General orientation defects.
5. Disorders of attention (e.g., short attention span, distractibility).
6. Impulsivity.
7. Disorders of memory and thinking.
8. Specific learning disabilities in reading, arithmetic, writing, and spelling.
9. Disorders of speech and hearing.
10. Equivocal neurological signs and electroencephalographic irregularities.

As with other complex conditions, continued experience with learning disabilities in children may reveal identifiable symptom complexes. At present we find few characteristics that are shared by all children identified as having learning disabilities. Kirk's definition in Chapter 1 suggests three common elements among all such children:

1. *All are retarded or disordered in school subjects, speech or language and/or manifest behavior problems.* The terms *retarded* and *disordered* suggest a discrepancy between the child's expected performance and his actual performance, but they differ in their educational consequences. A retardation or delay suggests a slow rate of advancement toward educational goals. Disorder, conversely, suggests malfunction and indicates either remedial or (failing that) circumventive procedures. It is possible that a disordered child may never achieve minimal educational goals, while a retarded child may

achieve such goals in time. The distinction has educational value.

The inclusion of speech and language as characteristics that may be retarded or disordered effectively makes it possible to identify many children with learning disabilities at the preschool level. Manifest speech and language problems in preschoolers may or may not be accompanied by some of the other characteristics listed by Clements. They may or may not be a sign of learning disabilities. However, speech and language defects provide a possible sign of learning disabilities and incipient school problems. Moreover, clinical and psychometric techniques are available for assessing speech and language problems in children below school age. The importance of identifying preschoolers with possible learning disabilities via irregularities in speech and language development is clear.[2]

2. *None are assignable to major categories of exceptionality such as mental retardation or deafness.* The elimination of any major categories of exceptionality from consideration as a learning disability may be confusing. Mental retardation, for example, is ruled out—by definition—as a permissible cause for learning disabilities. It is still possible, however, for a mentally retarded child to have a learning disability if he has an educationally significant deviation among his own performances. Such a child may be performing, for example, two grades below normal for his life age because of his general intellectual deficit. If his reading performance were an additional grade and a half below his spelling, arithmetic, and writing, he could properly be regarded as having a learning disability in reading. None the less, he would be a mentally retarded child with a learning disability, not a child with a learning disability who was also mentally retarded. However, this distinction may be more semantic than real. Both the mentally retarded child with a specific learning disability in reading and the child with a learning disability who has reading problems may require similar educational remediation to elevate, or attempt to elevate, their reading performances. In fact, if the reading level and reading problems of such children are similar, common therapy may be appropriate. The goal of remediation would be to return each child to his appropriate functioning level in reading.

The presence of mental retardation, then, or any other major exceptionality such as deafness or blindness would preclude a child from being identified primarily as a child with a learning disability, by our definition.

3. *All have some presumed neurologic basis (cerebral dysfunction) for their manifest disability or disabilities.* This characteristic is the least relevant educationally and the most controversial generally. It must be admitted, however, that all other causes for learning disabilities appear to have been ruled out by the definition except, perhaps, emotional and social disturbance. And even here, it is reasonable to assume that Kirk, in his definition in Chapter 1, permits this as a cause of learning disabilities in order to identify those among the socially and emotionally disturbed who have a neurologic basis for their behavior disabilities, for only such children are likely to profit from the basically pedagogical, non-affective remedial measures that Kirk proposes for children with learning disabilities.

Thus, identification of children with learning disabilities reduces to eliminating children whose behavior can be explained on a basis other than cerebral dysfunction. For the children surviving this elimination, some sort of cerebral dysfunction is presumed, to explain the learning deficit.

But cerebral dysfunction, presumed or real, is of little relevance to the educator. Of greater value to the special educator is the very process of eliminating other causes, not the inference of cerebral dysfunction itself. For in this process, many causes of aberrant behavior have already been eliminated and, with them, teaching techniques that could have been erroneously applied. There is positive value in knowing that a given child is not mentally retarded, not visually handicapped, and so on.

Thus, there are both idiosyncratic and common symptoms of learning disabilities. The former help distinguish one type of learning disability from another so that useful treatments can be prescribed to ameliorate the deficits. The latter help distinguish the child with learning disabilities from the child experiencing learning problems for other known reasons such as cultural disadvantage, inadequate instruction, or mental retardation.

ETIOLOGY

Minimal cerebral dysfunction[3] in the absence of frank disability is said to cause the behavioral manifestations responsible for learning disabilities.

Children designated as having minimal cerebral dysfunction, in the absence of neurological confirmation, may only be presumed to have actual dysfunction of the central nervous system. The behavior manifested by such children, often referred to as *organic*, is an observable fact. But the concept of organicity, according to Birch (1964), is not neurophysiologic, but behavioral. While evidence suggests that such behavior seldom exists in the absence of brain damage, organicity appears to be the consequence of certain types of brain damage "and should in no sense be mistaken as a prototype of disturbance which may accompany all instances of injury to the brain."[4] Thus, cerebral dysfunction is complex and individualistic; its manifestations may depend on the locus, extent, and character of the dysfunction as well as the developmental stage during which the dysfunction originated and the nature of the causal agent(s).

Disturbed behavior is not the direct consequence of brain damage. Such behavior is the result of patterns developed "in the course of atypical relations with the developmental environment, including its interpersonal, objective, and social features," as noted by Birch.[5]

Not all types of cerebral dysfunction lead to learning disabilities or other manifestations of organicity in children. Conversely, not all learning problems in school are learning disabilities. Figure 1 depicts the situation.

Thus, presumed minimal cerebral dysfunction underlies the manifestations of organicity. These unusual behaviors, in intercourse with the environment, result in problems of an intellective and/or affective nature, both in and out of school (i.e., learning disabilities). Typically, cerebral dysfunction in children dates from events preceding or surrounding the birth process. Germ plasm defects, noxious influences and agents affecting the development of the embryo, fetus, or infant, and chemical or mechanical factors may damage, directly or indirectly, the delicate and irreplaceable neural tissue of the newborn. Traumatic, poisonous, or infectious factors may be responsible for postnatal cerebral insult. Verifiable neurological impairment, such as cerebral palsy, is known to be associated with a history of prematurity, anoxia, toxemia of pregnancy, Rh incompatibility, maternal rubella, or unusual delivery. In as many as one-third of the cases of verifiable neurological impairment the cause may be unknown. Minimal brain dysfunction

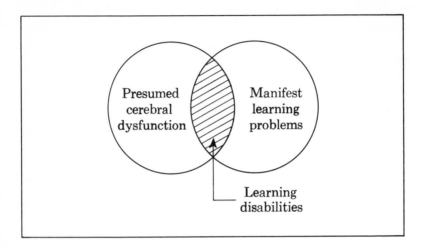

Learning
disabilities

FIGURE 1. The Locus of Learning Disabilities

such as is associated with learning disabilities "may arise from
genetic variations, biochemical irregularities, perinatal brain insults,
illnesses or injuries sustained during the years critical for the development and maturation of the central nervous system or from
unknown causes."[6] Unlike Kirk, Clements does not eliminate the
possibility that severe, early sensory deprivation results in subtle but
permanent alterations in the central nervous system. Often the history of the child with actual neurological impairment will reveal
events that are presumed to be associated with the central nervous
system damage. But such events are also associated with the histories of children with minimal cerebral dysfunction.

Conventional neurological examinations frequently reveal little
that is clearly abnormal in children with learning disabilities. Some
of the more revealing tests include manual dexterity and visual
motor coordination; hand, eye, and foot dominance; sensory testing; and evaluation of tendon reflexes and plantar responses (see
Paine, 1965). None the less, even very careful and detailed neurological study will often not differentiate such children from the
non-neurologically impaired, and psychological tests of perception,
memory, praxia, speech, and language are ordered. Establishing
the neurological basis for minimal cerebral dysfunction is a complex

process. The interested reader is referred elsewhere for technical detail. (See Kennedy and Ramirez, in Birch, 1964; also pp. 173-183 in Birch, 1964.)

EPIDEMIOLOGY

Epidemiology is more than the study of the number of cases of given diseases in a population. It involves an attempt to explain those forces that tend to increase or decrease prevalence rates. The lack of an exclusive definition of children with learning disabilities precludes a precise consideration of epidemiology or even prevalence rates in this area. However, Gruenberg (in Birch, 1964) has made a number of observations on the subject, which are useful and have been summarized below. The interested reader is referred to the original source for the complete text of this excellent article. Gruenberg distinguishes among three types of children who may manifest the symptoms of brain injury: (1) those with established neurological impairment, (2) those with purely functional impairment, and (3) those with suspected but unconfirmed neurologic impairment (organoid). The prevalence of school-age children in each category is speculative. Children with established neurological impairment (e.g., cerebral palsy, epilepsy) account for one percent or less of the school-age population. Children with functional (learned) defects would form a substantial portion of the school-age population if we included among them the educationally retarded and culturally disadvantaged. Such children may have educational disabilities but not learning disabilities. Fifteen to twenty percent of the school-age population probably would not be too great an estimate of the prevalence of this group. Organoid children, as Gruenberg defines them, are similar to children with learning disabilities as we have described them in the preceding section on etiology. Their prevalence is unknown but estimates of five percent of the school-age population (and higher) are not uncommon.

Our particular interest is in Gruenberg's organoid group, for here we find the "soft" neurological signs and the specific learning deficits. In his discussion of epidemiology, Gruenberg observed that many of these children come from the families of the poor and, from this view, posits three theories which might account for that observation:[7]

1. The Eugenical.—Like beget like, and if the unfit stopped begetting, the numbers of unfit would decline.
2. The Social Darwinist.—The poor are poor because they are poor biological stuff. To the fittest go the rewards.
3. The Euthenical.—The poor are handicapped because their living conditions are undesirable; if they had a better environment, the number of cases would drop.

These theories are not mutually exclusive. But among and between them are included all essential elements for theorizing on the issue. Of course, to the degree that the "premise of poorness" is in error, these theories will miss the mark.

Gruenberg supplements these theories with two observations: 1. From data on the mentally retarded (this group will include some of the organoid children), a sharp decrease in prevalence is noted after the chronological age of thirteen.

2. The disease prevalence rate is higher for boys than girls.

The dramatic drop in prevalence of retardation originating in the early teen period could be accounted for, according to Gruenberg, by (1) regarding the school as a sort of case finding agency, (2) high mortality rates, and (3) a "schoologenic hypothesis." This latter is regarded as the most likely explanation of the phenomenon. It derives from the notion of a "functional disequilibrium between the individual and his environment; we take it for granted that society assigns roles in a reasonable way and that those who fail to fulfill roles have something wrong with them. I think we have grounds for questioning this assumption."[8] Since the society into which the retardate returns is less discriminating about intellectual performance than the specific portion of society called the school, many considered retarded by school standards will be considered basically non-retarded by general societal standards. This reasoning is buttressed by the fact that the incidence of retardation below school age is also quite low. This phenomenon is common to most countries where records are available. By analogy, Gruenberg suggests the same is true for the organoid child. Convincing as this case is, it does not preclude the possibility of alterations in physiologic function in puberty, or at least some combination of such alterations interacting with "schoologenic" features. Though little has been reported as yet on the adolescence and adulthood of children with learning disabilities, clinical reports seem to suggest the possibility of alterations of brain-injury symptoms with age.

There is a large sex difference in disease prevalence, and in fact Gruenberg feels the excess of males with defects is underestimated. Several theories (e.g., larger head size, resulting in more birth injuries, sex-linked susceptibility) can collectively account for the boy-girl discrepancy, but no single theory can adequately explain it. The general line of evidence, according to Gruenberg, suggests environmental factors at work. And this suggests the topic of prevention.

The most fruitful approach to prevention lies in an attack on unfavorable maternal, fetal, and infant environments. Gruenberg feels that children currently regarded as organoid are so due largely to preventable causes. But he reminds us that while improved environments will lead to a reduced prevalence of brain damage in children, it will also assist the survival of handicapped individuals, thereby raising the prevalence again.

One must conclude that the forces that account for the prevalence of learning disabilities are largely inferred and speculative at this time, deriving from theory and by analogy from data on other diseases. But it is clear that epidemiological data for this type of child are required for their explanatory power and for the viable suggestions for treatment, care, and prevention they would make possible. First, however, a broadly acceptable definition of learning disabilities is required.

REFERENCES

1. Sam D. Clements, *Minimal Brain Dysfunction in Children*, NINDB Monograph No. 3, Public Health Service Bulletin No. 1415 (Washington D.C.: U.S. Dept. of Health, Education, and Welfare, 1966b) p. 13.
2. Just such a study is underway by Ryckman and others at the University of Michigan. (Personal correspondence.)
3. Brain-damage, neurologic impairment and (minimal) cerebral dysfunction have all been used in the literature on learning disabilities. In the present book they are used interchangeably. Cerebral dysfunction is, perhaps, the safest term to use. It does not necessarily imply physical damage to the brain; it simply describes a brain that is not functioning properly.
4. Herbert G. Birch, ed., *Brain Damage in Children* (Baltimore: Williams and Wilkins Co., 1964) p. 7.

5. BIRCH, *Brain Damage in Children*, p. 8.
6. CLEMENTS, Abstract in *Special Education: Strategies for Educational Progress*, 44th CEC Convention papers, pp. 188-189.
7. ERNEST M. GRUENBERG, "Some Epidemiological Aspects of Congenital Brain Damage," in *Brain Damage in Children*, Herbert G. Birch, ed. (Baltimore: Williams and Wilkins Co., 1964) p. 120. Courtesy, Association for the Aid of Crippled Children, New York, N.Y.
8. GRUENBERG, *Brain Damage in Children*, pp. 122-3.

3

DIFFERENTIAL DIAGNOSIS

It is axiomatic that remedial procedures based upon gross or inaccurate diagnosis will not yield optimal results. Consequently, an adequate diagnosis is critically important. Moreover, the diagnosis must not only distinguish the child with learning disabilities from the child with categorical disabilities (e.g., mental retardation, deafness), but it must suggest a course of action for the educator even as a knowledge of etiology suggests a course of action for the physician. We can refer to this highly skilled activity as *differential diagnosis*.

Unfortunately, among children with learning disabilities similar symptoms can arise from diverse causes. For example, the failure of language to appear at the expected age may be symptomatic of deafness, mental retardation, emotional disturbance, aphasia, or a subtle cerebral dysfunction. Therapeutic procedures instituted on the assumption of emotional disturbance in a child who is actually hard of hearing cannot be expected to yield more than a fortuitous gain. The remedy must fit the defect. The problem is to diagnose adequately the defect.

Success in educational diagnosis cannot depend upon the determination of etiology, because in children with learning disabilities etiology is usually presumed. While presumption of etiology does not prevent an adequate diagnosis of educational problems, it complicates matters by requiring the treatment of symptoms. In stuttering, for example, where etiology is usually presumed, the treatment of symptoms is routinely undertaken. Thus, though the theoretical causes of stuttering differ widely, the course of treatment is largely the same regardless of theoretical orientation.

But among children with learning disabilities where, unlike stutterers, symptoms differ widely, treatment seems very much hinged to the theoretical assumptions about the root cause of the disability. Thus, presumed etiology is not the only pitfall associated with differential diagnosis. Assuming all symptoms are associated with a common theoretical cause is another.

A diagnosis of learning disabilities is often indicated by systematically ruling out other causative factors. In the process of distinguishing the child with learning disabilities from his counterpart with a categorical disability, the diagnostician verifies that the child's primary deficit is not mental retardation, hearing impairment, emotional problems, or the like. This diagnosis-by-elimination is scientifically untenable because the explanation of "what is not causing the problem" is not the same as the disclosure of "what is causing the problem." In addition, if etiology must be presumed, the clinician may use the treatment itself as part of a continuing diagnosis, on the assumption that if treatment fails to show results in time, then an inappropriate surmise about the etiology of the defect might have been made in the first place. There are some obvious weaknesses in this reasoning, since the child could improve for reasons unassociated with treatment or could fail to improve, though the treatment be appropriate, for a variety of reasons (e.g., poorly executed remedial procedures). Thus, at this state of the art, the need for observational skill, valid and reliable testing instruments, and superbly trained clinicians is apparent.

For the specialist who can tolerate ambiguity and maintain flexible and critical surveillance of behavior, this approach does provide a modus operandi. But it is not difficult, under the circumstances, to understand the present lack of professional consensus on definition and treatment of children with learning disabilities when the critical process of differential diagnosis is characterized by (a) presumed etiology deriving from "diagnosis-by-elimination," (b) the treatment of symptoms, (c) treatments which derive from any of a variety of theoretical frameworks, and (d) treatment which is validated by improvement in performance. Perhaps

Clements' (1966b) *diagnostic evaluation* is a more suitable term for what we do than *differential diagnosis*.

Clements[1] has produced a set of guidelines for examining children with learning disabilities, which are given below. Here is a wide ranging, "buckshot" search for defects, which may serve as a basis for assessing behavior and provide a key for subsequent treatment.

GUIDELINES FOR THE DIAGNOSTIC EVALUATION OF DEVIATING CHILDREN

A. Medical Evaluation

1. Histories

a. *Medical*—To include pre-, peri-, and post-natal information. Details of all childhood illnesses should be obtained, including age of child at time of illness, symptoms, severity, course, and care (such as physician in attendance, hospitalization).

b. *Development*—To include details of motor, language, adaptive, and personal-social development.

c. *Family-Social*—To involve parents, child, and others as indicated. The family-social history should include detailed information regarding family constellation, acculturation factors, specific interpersonal family dynamics, emotional stresses, and traumata.

2. Physical Examination

a. *General*—To evaluate general physical status and to search for systemic disease. The physical examination should be done as part of the current evaluation of the child, and not obtained at a previous time for some other purpose, e.g., routine preschool checkup or in conjunction with a previous illness. Many child study clinics obtain a report on the "physical status" of the child from the family physician or pediatrician as a part of the referral policy. It is not uncommon, however, for the physician simply to fill out the requested form from his records on the child without conducting a current examination.

b. *Neurologic*—To evaluate neurological function and to search for specific disorders of the nervous system. The developmental aspects of neurologic integration assume primary importance for this examination, especially with reference to integrated motor acts, as opposed to simple reflexes.

3. Special Examinations

   a. *Ophthalmologic*—To include visual acuity, fields, and fundi examinations.
   b. *Otologic*—To include audiometric and otoscopic examinations.

4. Routine Laboratory Tests

   a. *Serologic*
   b. *Urinalysis*
   c. *Hematologic*

5. Special Laboratory Tests (only when specifically indicated)

   a. *Electroencephalographic*—To include wake, sleep, and serial tracings.
   b. *Radiologic*
   c. *Pneumoencephalographic*
   d. *Angiographic*
   e. *Biochemical*
   f. *Genetic assessment: Chromosome analysis*

B. Behavioral Assessment

1. *Academic History:* To involve child's teachers and principal, their observations regarding school behavior as well as academic progress and achievement. The child's school records, including samples of schoolwork and test results, should be available to the diagnostic team.
2. *Psychological Evaluation:* (The following items represent the core of the psychological evaluation.)
   a. Individual comprehensive assessment of intellectual functioning.
   b. Measures of complex visual-motor-perceptual functioning.
   c. Behavioral observations in a variety of settings.
   d. Additional indices of learning and behavior as indicated.
3. *Language Evaluation:* Detailed assessment of speech and language behavior. To include audiometric screening; assessment of articulation, voice quality, and rate; and the expressive and receptive aspects of language.
4. *Educational Evaluation:* An educational diagnostician should conduct detailed analyses of academic abilities, including achievement assessment for details of levels and methods of skill acquisition; e.g., reading, number concepts, spelling and writing.

These guidelines reveal the extraordinary diversity and wide scope of inquiry. The educator is concerned chiefly with the behavioral assessment, particularly the psychological, linguistic, and educational aspects. The remainder of this chapter will be devoted to a consideration of some current diagnostic tools and approaches.

Psychological Evaluation

The three areas of major concern in psychological evaluation are intellectual, visual-motor-perceptual, and personality functioning.

Intelligence tests. When tested with standard individual intelligence tests (e.g., Binet, 1960) unremarkable results are often obtained. Typically, children with learning disabilities range between low average to average in intelligence. While this distinguishes them from the mentally retarded, it also forms one basis for their learning disability, for it is the discrepancy between the mental age obtained on the intelligence test and the grade achievement scores (obtained on achievement tests) that is a benchmark of learning disabilities. Test batteries composed of several subtests, such as the Wechsler Intelligence Test for Children (WISC, 1949) or Wechsler Preschool and Primary Scale of Intelligence (WPPSI, 1967) have been preferred, since the discrepancy among subtests scores can suggest the basis for further testing, and, perhaps, avenues for remediation. But subtest scatter, while useful in remediation, is not especially useful as a diagnostic sign, because it will not always distinguish the child with learning disabilities from children with other conditions, such as mental retardation.

There is a host of intelligence tests available to the psychologist, but the WISC and Binet are among the most reliable and useful of these instruments. Generally they present no major problems of administration, and they do not rely excessively upon visual-motor-perceptual abilities, abilities often said to be impaired in children with learning disabilities.

Visual-motor-perceptual tests. The observation that visual-motor-perceptual abilities may be impaired in children with learning disabilities dates from before Strauss and has been utilized in the construction of numerous tests such as the Bender Visual-Motor Gestalt Test (1962), the Benton Visual Retention Test (1955), the Graham-Kendall Memory-for-Designs Test (1960), the Syracuse Visual Figure Background Test (1957), and the informal Kephart tests found in his textbook *The Slow Learner In the Classroom.*

Children with established neurological impairment often perform in deviant manners on these tests; children with learning disabilities often perform in a similar way. Such tests, by themselves, are not infallible indicators of the existence of learning disabilities, because not all such children perform deviantly on these tests. Indeed, not all frankly neurologically impaired children show impaired performance on these tests.

Another common observation is that children with learning disabilities are often unable to recall and reproduce a sequence of numbers, letters, or non-meaningful symbols although many of these same children can correctly repeat meaningful symbol sequences such as sentences.

Personality tests. It is important to make a distinction between the impulsive and disinhibited behavior exhibited by some children with learning disabilities and the acting-out and aggressive behavior sometimes exhibited by children with behavioral problems. The value of the differential diagnosis lies in the assignment of remedial measures. The treatment of a child with suspected cerebral dysfunction would differ, presumably, from the therapeutic measures accorded a child with 'purely' affective disorders. Of course, this distinction may be a precious one. Future research may show that the same therapies will benefit optimally both types of child. Now, however, this would appear to be an oversimplified view. Since the child with learning disabilities has no frank sensory defects, there are no limitations on the kinds of assessment techniques that are accorded him in the affective areas. Normed tests, such as the California Test of Personality (1953), clinical tests such as the Children's Apperception Test (1961), scales like the Vineland Social Maturity Scale (1953), psychiatric workups, and observations have all been employed. As in so many other instances, results distinguish the child with learning disabilities from the normal child but not from children with other kinds of handicaps. This, then, is one of the hard empirical facts that makes characterizing children with learning disabilities so difficult—they are difficult to distinguish, on the basis of psychological testing, from other handicapped children.

Linguistic Evaluation

Linguistic ability, as used here, refers to the ability to communicate and think in language symbols. Speech is regarded simply as the articulation of sounds and sound patterns. It is possible for a child to have language and speech problems, speech problems alone, or language problems alone.

Linguistic performance is often affected in the child with learning disabilities. On tests like the Peabody Picture Vocabulary Test (PPVT, 1959) the Illinois Test of Psycholinguistic Abilities (ITPA, 1961; 1968) and on classic measures of language ability such as sentence complexity, children with learning disabilities not only tend to score lower than normal children but are often quite discrepant in their performance on tests of various abilities that contribute to overall language performance. Such children, for example, might be average for their age on tests of receptive language ability but below average on tests of expressive language ability.

Language is perhaps one of the most sensitive indicators of inner states in man, and it seems to be affected by defects and disequilibria of all kinds. Thus, while children with learning disabilities often have linguistic impairments, this is not a distinctive indicator of the learning disability because it is a widely shared symptom. Even subtest patterns on test batteries like the ITPA may not reliably distinguish children with learning disabilities from children with other types of problems. But given that (a) the diagnosis of learning disabilities can be established on the basis of tests and other psychological data, and (b) there is value in treating symptoms directly, tests like the ITPA are useful in remediation as well as diagnosis. This will be discussed further in the sections on Bateman and Wiseman in the following chapter.

Children typically develop the ability to talk and to understand speech as preschoolers. Linguistic defects detected at an early age can often be remediated prior to entrance into school and the detrimental effects of such problems on secondary linguistic skills (e.g., reading, writing, spelling) precluded or reduced. The logical relationship between speaking and understanding speech and writing and reading is supported by the consistent appearance in the research literature of large and positive correlations between language ability and intelligence, and between language ability and academic achievement (McCarthy, 1964). In fact, there is some reason to believe that these correlations may be causal. If this can be experimentally established, not only could early linguistic skills be seen as precursors of subsequent complex linguistic skills, but intelligence and achievement in school could be viewed as a function of linguistic ability. Improvements in linguistic ability could lead to improvements in intellectual function and school achievement. To the degree that such speculation is accurate, linguistic remediation may be looked upon as a tool for the improvement of intellectual and academic capability, a lead of great significance, particularly in children whose problems are characterized by intellectual and academic impairment. Kirk (1966) has utilized precisely this approach with some success among school-age mentally retarded children. A complete presentation can be found in *Diagnostic Remediation of Psycholinguistic Abilities*. Thus, differential diagnosis and remediation of linguistic defects, especially at a preschool level, appears to be of substantial value.

Of course, numerous clinical efforts have been made to assess and remediate a host of learning problems in preschoolers. The argument that prior defects lead to subsequent school failures is powerful. Haeussermann (1958), from many years of clinical experience with preschool mentally retarded and/or brain-damaged children, has evolved an educational evaluation that attempts to detect weaknesses in educationally significant areas such as immediate recall, memory, presence of mind, and frustration tolerance. From the logical standpoint and from research, one can demonstrate the involvement of linguistic abilities even in skills such as these. It is, no doubt, the pervasive character of language ability in human behavior that accounts for its involvement in the differential diagnosis and remediation of learning disabilities.

Educational Evaluation

Among the academic skills that are most notably deficient in children with learning disabilities, reading seems to hold a primary position. Accordingly, diagnostic reading tests such as Durrell's (1945), Spache's (1955), and Monroe's (1935), are frequently used in the assessment of school-age children. Indeed, it is often inappropriately low reading performance, as contrasted with achievement in other academic skills, that is a principal clue in identifying a child with learning disabilities. Of course, not all poor readers have learning disabilities as we have defined them. But many children with learning disabilities in whom poor reading is a symptom, lack those automatic skills such as sound blending, visual closure, and retention of non-meaningful stimuli sequences that are associated with reading, while they perform reasonably well on the more meaningful aspects of the reading process. Such children, for instance, may be able to repeat a sentence of ten words but not be able to repeat a three-number sequence. Procedures to attempt to develop these automatic skills as well as remedial reading techniques (Fernald, 1943; Monroe, 1932; Gillingham and Stillman, 1960) have been used with some success.

Achievement tests covering the bulk of academic skills (e.g., Wide Range Achievement Test, 1946) are often employed to establish the discrepancy among academic skills that characterizes the child with learning disabilities. Myklebust has written a book, *Development and Disorders of Written Language*, Vol. I, which describes the Picture Story Language Test and its use in the differential diagnosis of children on the basis of their written output. Little has been written about the performance of children with learning disabilities in arithmetic or spelling, but presumably some of the same difficulties in learning that impair their linguistic performance impair, to the degree in which they are involved, their output in spelling and arithmetic.

Clearly, it is desirable to detect children with learning disabilities as early as possible. Not only can subsequent academic failure be avoided or lessened, but remediation (other things being equal) should be more readily and permanently accomplished.

Assessment Through Behavior Modification Techniques

A promising approach to assessment and remediation is emerging in the field of behavior modification. In this approach, baseline data on the defective behavior are collected over a period of time. This is followed by an assessment of those behavioral components that maintain and modify the child's behavior. According to Lovitt (1967), the study of these components includes a knowledge of antecedent or stimulus events (subject preferences), response behaviors, the design of contingency systems, and assessment of the environmental consequences that maintain behavior. When these data are obtained for a given individual, modifications can proceed. If behavior can be treated directly, without concern for its etiology, some of the more troublesome issues raised in the beginning of this chapter can be eliminated.

One of the obvious advantages of this approach is the highly personalized nature of the data obtained for each subject in the course of his remediation. What motivates the student and precisely how he responds to this motivation is important. No assumptions are made, or need to be. Another advantage is the possibility of the direct intervention of the teacher in the diagnostic and remedial processes. Doubtless the disadvantages of behavior modification will become apparent as its use increases with children having learning disabilities. However, this approach seems uniquely rooted in human behavior and is not encumbered with models from medicine and the physical sciences.

It is probably incorrect to perceive behavior modification techniques as independent of and apart from the more traditional psychometric approaches. Lovitt's discussion of the total process of assessment brings these approaches into a comprehensive relationship, and is recommended to the interested reader.

REFERENCES

1. CLEMENTS, *Minimal Brain Dysfunction in Children*, pp. 14-15. This is the first of three task force reports for the Department of Health, Education and Welfare on the topic of learning disabilities.

4

EDUCATIONAL PROCEDURES

For the educator, a discussion of children with learning disabilities begins logically with Strauss and his co-workers. In describing his work at Cove Schools (Strauss and Lehtinen, 1947), Strauss clearly identified the behavior we associate today with learning disabilities. In separate chapters he wrote about the child with "pathology of perception," "pathology of language," "pathology of concept formation," and "pathology of behavior." In the same book, Lehtinen related these behaviors to the problems of education. In a sense, subsequent work has been largely refinements of the treatments of these behaviors. Since Strauss, controversies have arisen about whether or not these behaviors are, or need be, associated with cerebral dysfunction and how best to educate such children, but there is no disagreement regarding the behaviors he described.

Kephart's subsequent work (1960) further elaborated the role of response in the total learning process, though there is some doubt as to whether Kephart was addressing himself to the same type of child as he was in his earlier collaboration with Strauss. Barsch (1965) refined the role of motion (dynamics of response), with particular stress on ocular mechanisms. His earlier work at the Cove Schools is reflected in the Movigenic Theory.

Frostig (1964) and the Fitzhughs (1966) are not lineal descendants of Strauss's thinking though they have concentrated their efforts on the perceptual problems, which have become a bench-mark of Strauss's work and the most universally acknowledged characteristic of children with learning disabilities.

One of the more controversial approaches is that taken by Delacato (1963). Assuming a rather direct relationship between defective performance and a defective nervous system, he has undertaken to modify the nervous system by carefully controlling the child's performance. The controversiality of this approach does not stem from the assumption of the relationship of behavior to neural events, but rather from the assumption that certain exter-nally imposed exercises can alter neural events in predictable ways.

Because the "pathology of language" identified by Strauss has also been identified with learning disabilities, certain approaches to linguistic remediation have been recruited to the list of tech-niques employed in the education of children with learning dis-abilities. The work of Bateman (1964) and Wiseman (1965) will be considered in this regard.

Associated also with methodology used with learning disabilities are some of the remedial approaches to education (e.g., Orton, 1937; Fernald, 1943) that predate Strauss and were found appli-cable to children with learning problems long before we had a label for such children.

These efforts, and other supportive works, will be discussed in the following chapter. The reader will note some striking similar-ities among methods, despite the fact that these are arrived at from differing theoretical points of departure. Perhaps the chief com-munality among approaches is the uniform need for the experi-mental verification of efficacy.

PERCEPTUAL-MOTOR APPROACHES

Alfred Strauss and Laura Lehtinen

Strauss* acknowledged two sources as the starting points for his deliberations—the early philosophy of corrective education of the mentally retarded,[1] and the work on brain injury in adults. Itard and Seguin came in for special mention for their work with the

---

* From Alfred A. Strauss and Laura Lehtinen, *Psychopathology and Educa-tion of the Brain-Injured Child,* 1947. Courtesy Grune and Stratton, New York.

retarded, and Kurt Goldstein for his work with brain-injured adults. One of Strauss's own contributions was isolating the exogenous retardate (later, brain-injured child) and relating his psychopathological characteristics to those of the traumatically brain-injured adults. Later it was noted that the symptomatology of brain injury was not confined to a restricted region of the IQ scale. Strauss noted, "Since clinical and psychological examination yielded similar results with all types of brain-injured children irrespective of their placement on the Binet scale of intelligence, the syndrome of exogeneity was extended to the clinical label of the 'brain-injured'."[2]

Strauss's explanation of the effects of brain damage in children derived from his training in child psychiatry and neurology. According to Lehtinen:[3]

. . . He rejected much of the then-current thinking in neurology as inappropriate for the diagnosis of children's learning and behavior disorders, strongly maintaining that a science of adult neurology was inadequate for the understanding of childhood deviations. His studies in neuropathology convinced him that the brain damages of the perinatal period were frequently the result of small diffuse hemorrhages scattered throughout the brain and that their effect would be apparent in disturbances of total brain function expressed in behavior and learning problems rather than in specific localizing neurological signs. Pediatric neurology as a specialty was unknown at that time and Strauss devised an outline for a pediatric neurological examination that relied on the presence of minor neurological signs. He was firmly convinced of the totality of brain function and of the essential inseparability of input and output (receptive and expressive) mental activity. He viewed the educative process for the brain-injured child as:

a. providing for the child an opportunity to experience the normalcy of being able to focus attention undisturbed by external distractions, and feel the closure of insight and understanding, in the expectation that he would wish for and seek to duplicate this experience;

b. strengthening through practice with specially selected and prepared materials those areas of function in which weaknesses existed which interfered with the total learning progression;

c. teaching compensations or detours if the usual input or expressive processes were severely impaired.

The child was always observed as an individual with a personality and mental endowment which was uniquely his and which provided the broad boundary within which the educator's work needed to be done. Because of the many dimensions resulting from the child's chronological age, life experiences, inherited mental abilities, temperament, personality and motivations, as well as the disabling effects of his brain damage no method or single approach was ever regarded as sufficient for every child. The educational approach consisted in a knowledge of normal child development, an understanding of the impairments and disruptions related to the brain damage, sensitive observation of the child's performance and analysis of his failure, and finally, a decision as to an appropriate procedure for improving the performance. The latter might be one which had been used successfully with other children with similar problems or it might be an original one improvised for a particular child. With this educational philosophy, the teacher's capacity to observe and analyze was constantly challenged and her energies directed toward creative solutions for the child's learning difficulties.

Four criteria were employed by Strauss to distinguish the *brain-injured child*:

1. The medical history should show evidence of injury to the brain by trauma or inflammatory processes before, during, or after birth.
2. The presence of slight neurological signs, which may indicate a brain lesion.
3. If the psychological disturbance is of such severity that retardation of intellectual growth is observed, the immediate family history must be essentially normal and indicate that he is the only one of the sibship thus afflicted.
4. When no mental retardation exists, the presence of psychological disturbances can be discovered by the use of certain qualitative tests for perceptual and conceptual disturbances.

Strauss noted that even if the first three signs were negative, the diagnosis of brain injury might still be considered. Indeed, the diagnosis of learning disabilities today relies largely on the fourth of these criteria.

In a series of studies Strauss attempted to differentiate the exogenous from the endogenous child, and having to his satisfaction done so, proceeded to list and discuss the peculiar learning problems of the brain-injured child and educational approaches to these problems.

Perception, a process midway between sensation and thought, was often disturbed in the brain-injured child. Strauss drew upon his background in Gestalt psychology to explain the basis of perceptual defects, and indeed to test for and remediate such defects. Excellent summaries of Gestalt theory are available elsewhere (e.g., Osgood, 1953; pp. 200-208). Certain fundamental dynamics were posited by Gestalt psychologists and demonstrated through a series of experiments, chiefly in visual perception. In substance, a "visual field" exists in which events follow certain rules under normal circumstances. Like processes in this field are said to attract one another. The more these forces are qualitatively similar, or the closer they are in time or space, the more likely they are to attract one another.

Look at Figure 2. What do you see? The standard answer is "a cross." Perhaps you also see four squares, as an afterthought. Here

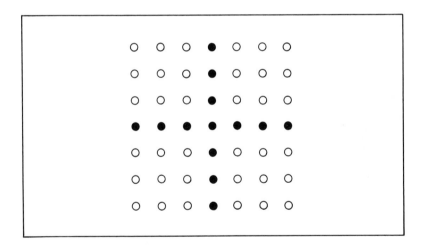

FIGURE 2. An Illustration of Cohesive Forces

similar elements are unified into a figure because of the underlying "cohesive forces" between the similar elements. The transition from such an example to Strauss's marble-board test is fairly direct.

A certain amount of perceptual lability is present in normal perception. For example, Figure 3 could be a piece of paper with

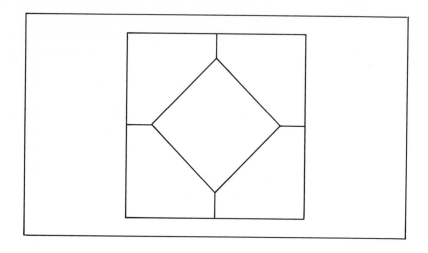

FIGURE 3. An Illustration of Foreground-Background Lability

a diamond-shaped hole cut in it, or a square hole in the wall through which you are viewing a cube suspended by strings from its corners. What you see depends upon what section of the figure you identify as foreground and what you identify as background. Brain-injured children were believed to have excessive foreground-background difficulty, as indexed by their ineptness on foreground-background tests created by Strauss and his co-workers. These examples of the Straussian application of Gestalt psychology to the testing of perceptual disturbances are oversimplified, but they do represent the basis for the introduction of these and similar techniques into the field of learning disabilities. Tactile and auditory perceptual problems were also identified in such children, but techniques for testing were not as well developed. Of course, not all symptoms (e.g., perseveration, distractibility, rigidity) would be predicted by Gestalt psychology, although once clinically observed, all could be explained. From the perceptual standpoint then, the brain-injured child was one who did not "follow the perceptual rules."

But Strauss found, in addition, unusual conceptual behavior among his exogenous children. Given a large number of objects to sort into groups on the basis of common characteristics, unusual combinations would result based upon form, color, or unessential detail. When asked to rationalize the basis of the grouping, the child provided far-fetched connections or relationships based upon a hypothetical or imaginary situation. Strauss noted, too, the tendency to "go off" on another line of thinking during sorting, and to be very meticulous in the placement of objects in groups. He noted that such behavior had its parallel in studies of brain-injured adults.

Perhaps the most striking manifestations of Strauss's children were their behavior disorders. The characteristics associated with some of the children included hyperactivity, distractibility, disinhibition, and perseveration. The occurrence of these symptoms is individualistic. Strauss repeatedly stressed the necessity to tie observations to the child's level of development—some of the "pathological" symptoms may be quite normal in young children. A chief problem was to distinguish brain-injury behavior from psychosis, neurosis, and schizophrenia, because of common symptoms. Clinical evidence is presented by Strauss to demonstrate that such distinctions are possible. For example, neurotic children manifest symptoms not typical of brain-injury such as tics, nail-biting, and anxieties.

Many of the educational measures suggested by Strauss were, in retrospect, attempts to overcome obstreperous symptoms of brain injury. Some related to Gestalt psychology and others were strictly Strauss. Great attention was paid to the characteristic distractibility of these children. As far as possible, all extraneous sights and sounds were eliminated. Rooms were spacious enough to accommodate a small group without crowding and were sparsely decorated. The lower panes of the windows were made translucent by being painted over. Often desks were faced to the wall or placed within an "office-like" furniture arrangement that further reduced extraneous visual stimuli. Kindergarten screens were used in some instances. Results were reported to be immediate—"the formerly unmanageable child becomes quite tractable."[4] Similarly, masking screens for printed matter, which permitted only small portions of a printed page to be viewed at one time were designed, thus doing away with the distraction provided by the print not actually being utilized at the moment. Principles of Gestalt psychology were used to direct learning via use of darkly outlining the "figure" area of materials or the use of color clues to attract attention to a given area. Motor activity, which assists in engaging the child to a task and holding his attention, was involved as much as possible. Distractibility and disinhibition are expressed motorically and can often be reduced by the channeling of motor activity. The utility of motor activity was mentioned profusely by Strauss but it was not until Kephart and Barsch that the implications of motor activity were fully appreciated.

The unsuitability of commercial instructional materials was noted by Strauss. Exercises were too complex and closely spaced, there was too much detail, and the rate of progress was inappropriate. Such materials had to be completely reworked. Where possible, Strauss urged his teachers to allow the child to assist in the construction of materials.

The instructional plan in the Cove Schools was limited to basic school skills and tended to be developmental for younger children and remedial for older ones. Typical "units" (e.g., the store, the post office) were not recommended for use with the brain-injured because of their many inherent distractions. Strauss emphasized the notion of his classrooms as INTERIM environments of a remedial or therapeutic nature. Children were returned ultimately to school classes (intellectually normal children to normal classes, retarded children to special classes for retardates, etc.). As a rule, drill was avoided because of the tendency of these children to automation, perseveration, and verbal memorization. The needed repetition was achieved through frequent experiences of insight and analyses, with drill following only after understanding was achieved. Great variability among children was common and the teacher learned to adjust her demands accordingly. The teaching of rhythm and manual training was recommended. Speech training, according to Strauss, was needed and should be done by specialists.

Clearly this was the first definitive work on the subject of educating brain-injured children. Remarkably innovative and insightful, Strauss had set the pattern for development of classes for brain-injured children and for children with what were to be called *learning disabilities*. With occasional exceptions or shifts in stress, this pattern largely dominates the thinking in the field today.

Newell Kephart

When Kephart completed his book, *The Slow Learner in the Classroom** in 1960, the term *learning disabilities* had not achieved prominence. Clearly, however, Kephart had identified and was attempting to solve the problems posed by those children who present marginal problems of classroom performance. These problems fall short of frank handicaps but are too debilitating to permit the child to progress through the grades without special assistance.

Kephart's insights come, in part, from his history of work with Strauss. Problems in these children are seen as largely perceptual-motor in nature and, consequently, remediation is aimed at those skills. Kephart holds that although the perceptual-motor problems are usually anatomical or physical in nature, they are aggravated or magnified by our restricted modern environment, in which children no longer have a need for, or adequate practice in, developing such basic abilities as eye-hand coordination, temporal-spatial translation, and form perception. Kephart feels these basic abilities relate to the types of achievement that schools demand.

The effects of the lack of exposure and practice on the central nervous system are dealt with on the level of behavioral psychology without a great deal of speculation about the role of specific brain mechanisms. However, to understand Kephart's remedial suggestions, some theoretical excursions into the organism are necessary. The explanation of feedback mechanisms in perception is a case in point. Figure 4 demonstrates how the muscular response of an organism is fed back into the total perceptual process to adjust the ultimate output. Other things being equal, the organism must respond for the adequate learning of basic skills to occur. For example, when a child traces a line and alters his movement, in direction and type, on the basis of visual information, feedback is being utilized. Or when a person throws a projectile at a target, feedback is involved. If the target is overthrown on the first attempt, muscular exertion is diminished on the second attempt. Thus, perceptual and motor learning proceed together, the response feeding back to correct the perception. Matters of body image, orientation in space, and discrimination hinge on this explanation.

---

* Newell C. Kephart, *The Slow Learner in the Classroom*, 1960. Courtesy Charles E. Merrill Books, Inc., Columbus, Ohio.

And to the degree that "higher" intellectual functions such as memory and concept formation depend upon adequacy of basic skills, they too can be expected to show corresponding deficits.

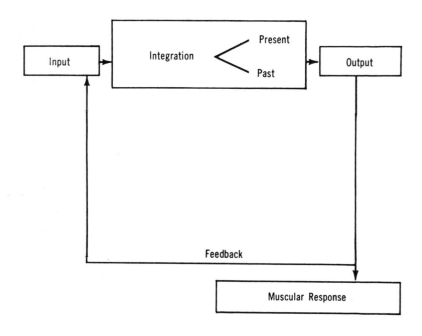

FIGURE 4. DIAGRAM OF FEEDBACK MECHANISM IN PERCEPTION

Kephart accepts the premise that if certain children lack the skills basic to school learning, the logical approach is to attempt to teach those skills. He created specific instructions for the development of form perception, space discrimination, form discrimination, ocular control, and sensory-motor integration. Kephart prefers to test children in their basic skill abilities and to regard progress as improvement in these abilities with time. A number of non-normed tests are suggested for this purpose (Kephart, 1960).

The Straussian heritage of Kephart is apparent in the implementation of ideas in the classroom, such as the use of chalkboard training, rail walking, balancing, ball play, tracing of templates, and music. Largely for theoretical reasons, the Kephart curriculum stresses the effects of movement on perception and the effects of perception on higher thought processes.

Kephart emphasizes the need to develop basic skills in their natural order of development. He stated, for example, that ". . . training is easier if it is begun with the most basic area of performance in which the child is weak."[5] Elsewhere, he discussed the dangers of splinter skills, that is, skills developed in advance of more basic skills. Because splinter skills have little generalizability, he believes they lead to no further development. The need to teach the child generalized skills is stressed by Kephart; teaching a specific task is always secondary. Frequent variations are always introduced to promote generalization.

Raymond Barsch

According to Barsch,* a curriculum for children with learning disabilities can have only one objective, namely, "to correct whatever impediments stand in the way of the child taking full advantage of the offerings of the regular curriculum."[6] Reasons for learning failure can be intellectual, psychiatric, or physiological. The deficits exhibited by children with learning disabilities cannot, as a rule, be explained as either basically intellectual or emotional defects; therefore, an explanation requires recourse to a consideration of the child as a sensory-perceptual-motor organism.

Like Kephart, Barsch accepts the view that because variations in such things as experiences, opportunities to learn, parental emphasis, and success level account for individual differences, they could also readily account for the type of manifestations associated with learning disabilities. Inasmuch as the "usual" curriculum has failed with such a child, an "unusual" curriculum is required; and since the root explanation of learning disabilities is seen by Barsch to lie not in the intellectual or affective realm, the appropriate curriculum would logically not emphasize these areas.

Movigenics is the study of the origin and development of movement patterns leading to learning efficiency. The movement theory,

---

* From Raymond H. Barsch, *A Movigenic Curriculum*, Madison, Wisc.: Bureau for Handicapped Children, 1965.

deriving from movigenics, is the basis for Barsch's physiologic curriculum. Eight major constructs form the core of the theory:[7]

1. All living organisms must survive in an energy surround. Radiant, mechanical and thermal energies represent the primary stimuli sources with which the organism must contend.
2. Survival in such an energy surround is contingent upon movement. The organism must move to survive. If movement cannot occur from independent initiation, the organism is at the mercy of the energy forces or dependently reliant upon others for survival.
3. The pull of gravity represents the major force to be resolved by the human organism in developing patterns of movements to promote survival. Independent control of gravitational force represents the most unique conflict confronting the human organism seeking identification in a world of erect-walking fellow beings. Building an adequate repertoire of movement patterns for survival in a variable, uncertain energy surround requires walking, crawling, hopping, running, squatting, rolling, etc.
4. The human organism may be defined as a homeostatic, adapting, bilaterally equating, dynamic, multistable system designed as an open energy mechanism so as to promote its survival in an energy surround.
5. Coordination is truly a matter of coordinates. Each individual builds a set of geometric coordinates within himself according to the patterns with which he learns to control his movement against gravitational pull and to center and align himself in a meaningful relationship to the energy surround in which he lives. Each individual resolves this battle in the most comforting manner possible even though this frequently requires that function alters structure and some penalty is accepted in lieu of full coordinative efficiency.
6. The terrain of movement is space. Each individual must organize a visual space volume, an auditory space volume, a tactual space volume and a kinesthetic space volume. These four modalities represent the major processing mechanisms utilized by the individual in moving to adapt to progressive daily demands. These are the volumes which must be organized for efficiency in movement. Failure to adequately organize each spatial volume results in some constricting penalty to the survival efficiency of the organism.
7. Movement has survival value to the human organism. When energy forces must be managed, informational data processed and behavior organized in ever increasing complexity, a program devoted to achieving optimal movement holds promise of making a significant contribution to learning efficiency.

8. Communication may be viewed as the expression of one's own "space world" in interchange with others. Various statements incorporated into language patterns may be cited as supporting this view as, "the way I see it," "from my point of view," "my viewpoint is," and many others of similar nature which suggest that the speaker is expressing a unique perception of his own. Communication then may be thought of as an interchange of "space worlds" between speakers, writer and reader, etc. The space world of an individual at any moment is composed of the totality of experiences available for expression. The manner in which the individual has been able to effectively process, organize and integrate all previous visual, auditory, kinesthetic and tactual information represents his communicative potential. Communication potential then becomes dependent upon the efficiency one holds in processing information from a variety of modality sources. Efficient patterns of movement then become crucial to communicative proficiency.

Using these constructs as a theoretical framework, Barsch developed the movigenic curriculum in which, through a planned program of activity, a child with a problem in learning receives an opportunity to explore and experience himself in space and is helped to integrate his experiences into progressively more complex relationships. Original sources (Barsch, 1965) must be consulted for more details and the practical implementation of movigenic theory. A brief description of an actual classroom, however, will provide some idea of the operationalization of movigenic theory. It should be emphasized that this is a description of a standard classroom modified to suit the program. Environment specifically built to accommodate this program would differ considerably from the standard classroom if all the constructs of movigenic theory were fully invoked.

Desks, books, and workbooks were removed to provide an open space for program use. All window panes were covered with black plastic sheeting, which allowed complete control of lighting. Lines painted on the floor marked where children were to be positioned for writing at the chalkboard, for transport routes, and other activities. A three-foot strip of carpeting was stretched across one end of the room to provide a surface for crawling and rolling. A variety of "alignment targets" was placed on vertical and horizontal surfaces. Children participated in all class sessions barefooted or in stocking feet. Teachers initially wore white blouses and black slacks, switching later to more colorful attire.

Some aspects of the program conducted in such classrooms provide further insight into the implementation of movigenic theory. No effort was made to follow a regular order of activity, although activities themselves were carefully planned. The purpose of this flexibility was to wean children from the need for a rigid schedule. Children were given a segment of visual information first through one eye, then the other, and then both eyes, while in various body positions. Auditory information was processed in an analogous manner. The use of darkness for flashlight tracking, relaxation, and auditory discrimination was a regular feature of the program. Emphasis was placed on regular parent counseling and staff conferences. The equipment used included a tachistoscope, walking and balancing rails, tracing templates, scooter and teeter boards, plastic balls of various sizes, a metronome, Cuisenaire rods, a geometric symbol system for reading, a stereoscope, and tape recorder. The use of teacher interns and one child helping another were part of the program.

Either the diagnostic-clinical approach or the intersensory apprenticeship approach can be used in remedial work. In the former approach, physical and psychological assessment is used to determine the specific strengths and weaknesses of the child, and remedial plans are cast on the basis of these findings. This is fairly standard practice. In the latter approach, children are exposed to all curricular activities and their level of performance noted. Progress in this case is measured by improvement in performance with time in these activities. The latter approach was preferred by Barsch.

One can identify the influence of Seguin, Montessori, and Strauss in Barsch's theory, along with ideas about movement and vision that seem quite novel. The effect of Barsch's work with Strauss and his experience as director of a special public-agency school for brain-injured children is evident in the detailed implementation of movigenic theory in the curriculum. Though many of the techniques are distinctly "Barsch," it is orientation to learning, rather than uniqueness or novelty, that characterizes his views.

Evidence directly supporting the efficacy of such an approach for children with learning disabilities is still largely clinical. One of the few existing studies (Painter, 1963) utilized this curriculum with 20 normal kindergarten children who represented the lower 50%

of a class of 40 on the basis of Goodenough mental age. The ten experimental children were given 21 half-hour sessions over a period of 7 weeks while the ten control children received no special training. Significant differences favoring the experimental group were reported in various sensory-motor skills and linguistic behavior. Apart from some design limitations, the small number of subjects and lack of follow-up restrict confidence in outcome. However, there seems to be sufficient promise to warrant further study. One suspects that a movigenic approach might work well with some children and not at all with others, depending on the cause of their inept school performance.

DEVELOPMENTAL APPROACHES IN VISUAL PERCEPTION

Marianne Frostig

Frostig's[*] published research and materials have focused primarily on assessment and remediation techniques in the area of visual perception. Her orientation derives largely from the developmental theories of Piaget and Werner, as well as from learning theory and psychoanalysis. Her Developmental Test of Visual Perception (1963)[8] evolved from clinical observations of children with learning difficulties, many of whom seemed to have disabilities in visual perception. The test was designed to serve as the basis of specific remedial programs; accordingly, the differentiation of various kinds of visual-perceptual abilities is one of its chief aims. Norms by age level are provided.

This paper and pencil test, standardized via group administration on a sample of over 2,100 Southern California children between the ages of 2½ and 9 years, assesses the five areas of visual perception described below. Children who score in the lowest quartile, as compared with their age-mates, may exhibit the difficulties listed.

NAME OF TEST	DESCRIPTION	MEASURES SUCH DIFFICULTIES AS:
I. Eye-Motor Coordination	Child draws straight or curved lines between increasingly narrow boundaries or draws a straight line to a target.	Inability to color within the lines of a figure.

[*] Courtesy Marianne Frostig, PhD, Marianne Frostig Center of Educational Therapy, Los Angeles, Cal.

FIGURE 5. Item 6 from Test I of the Developmental Test of Visual Perception

II. Figure-Ground   Child is asked to outline a specific form among intersecting shapes and to find hidden figures.   Finding words in a dictionary.

FIGURE 6. Item 4 from Test II of the Developmental Test of Visual Perception

III. Constancy of Shape   The task is to discriminate circles and squares in different shadings, sizes, and positions from other shapes on the page.   Failure to recognize a letter or word when written in different sizes, cases, or colors.

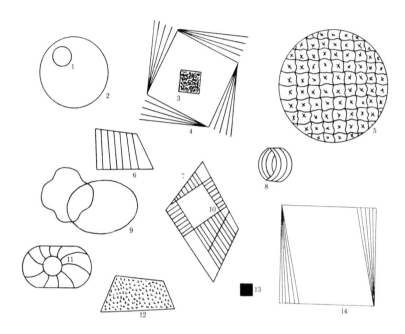

FIGURE 7. TEST III OF THE DEVELOPMENTAL TEST OF VISUAL
PERCEPTION

IV. Position in Space	Child differentiates between figures in an identical position and those in a reversed or rotated position.	Reversing letters or numbers.

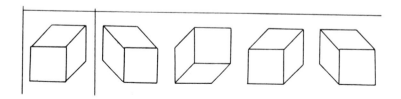

FIGURE 8. ITEM 8 FROM TEST IV OF THE DEVELOPMENTAL TEST
OF VISUAL PERCEPTION

| V. Spatial Relationships | The task is to copy patterns by linking dots. | Inability to put letters of a word in the proper order. |

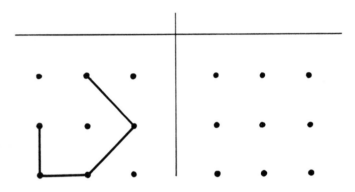

FIGURE 9. Item 6 from Test V of the Developmental Test of Visual Perception

Deficits in any of the areas tested may be referred to specially prepared exercises, specific to the problem discovered.

The visual perceptual training material developed by Frostig may serve (a) for ameliorating specific disabilities assessed by the test, and (b) as the focus for readiness training, which involves all abilities normally developed at the age of first school entrance.

At the Frostig Center of Educational Therapy, children with learning difficulties are evaluated in six developmental areas: sensory-motor abilities, language, visual and auditory perception, higher thought processes, social adjustment, and emotional development. Four tests are considered basic to instituting individualized remedial programs: Marianne Frostig's Development Test of Visual Perception (1964), Wepman's Auditory Discrimination Test (1958), Wechsler's Intelligence Scale for Children (1949), and the Illinois Test of Psycholinguistic Abilities (1961).

Frostig conceives the treatment of learning disturbances as a four-fold task: (1) amelioration of specific developmental lags,

primarily through programs focusing on these areas; (2) amelioration of global and pervasive disturbances, such as impulsivity and
distractibility, principally through techniques of classroom management; (3) teaching of subject matter and skills; and (4) aiding
the child's social adjustment and emotional development.

Kathleen and Loren Fitzhugh

Kathleen and Loren Fitzhugh* have contributed to the field of
visual-perceptual problems by producing a series of eight workbooks somewhat dissimilar in format, but similar in intent, to the
work of Frostig. The series, *The Fitzhugh Plus Program,* concen-
trates on two areas of learning: (1) spatial organization, and (2)
language and numbers.

The spatial organization exercises are an attempt to improve the
student's ability to perceive, comprehend, and manipulate shapes
or objects in space and time. The basic technique requires the
student to look at a figure in the left hand column and match it
with the proper one on the right hand side of the page. He marks
his choice with a special pencil and if the answer is correct, the
marking will turn green. The child is instructed to keep marking
until he gets the correct answer.

In the five language and numbers workbooks, the exercises are
designed to help the child improve his ability to identify letters,
numbers, words, and pictures as well as to increase understanding
of linguistic symbols and arithmetic operations. The marking procedure is the same as that used in the spatial organization workbooks.

The authors stated that work in these books should be limited
to about an hour a day and extended over a period of six months.
Testing before and after using the workbooks helps to indicate
whether or not they have contributed to educational growth.

The program does not claim to be a complete educational scheme
but rather a supplementary, remedial, or preparatory self-teaching
approach.

---

* From Kathleen B. and Loren Fitzhugh, *The Fitzhugh Plus Program,* 1966.
Courtesy Allied Education Council, Galien, Mich.

G. N. Getman

Getman* and his associates have developed a program of visuo-motor training based upon the belief that visual perception is learned (i.e., based upon developmental sequences of physiological actions) and that it evolves from actions of the entire organism. Furthermore, they believe it is necessary to have good coordination of the body parts and body systems in order to develop perception of forms and symbols.

To explain visual performance, Getman used Skeffington's diagram,[9] which shows four circles representing four performance areas merging at one central location into an emergent *vision*. The four performance areas are:

1. The Anti-Gravity Process, which is the total motor system used for locomotion, exploration, and organizing oneself in the environment. It is a combination of "modes of movement through space."
2. The Centering Process, which is the ability to place oneself and other things in the environment, to develop feelings of location and orientation.
3. The Identification Process, which is the ability to label things.
4. The Speech-Auditory Process, which is communication skill.

For Getman, there is a strong visual component to this last process, because he said we "take a look at" details to aid cognition. According to this theory, communication between individuals seems to involve trading or transferring visualizations. Also, he believed visualization cannot be acquired as a separate skill, that it must be achieved by the child out of his own systems. Merely finding new and interesting learning materials would not help the child unless the skill areas themselves were developed.

Skeffington's model explains visual performance, but does not show how perceptual skills develop, as does Getman's model of the visuomotor complex. This model is a guideline for mind-body training designed to assist children toward their maximum cognitive growth.

The first level of the model is labeled *Innate Response System*,[10] and Getman includes here the tonic neck reflex, the startle reflex,

---

* Permission granted by Special Child Publications, Inc., 4535 Union Bay Place, N.E., Seattle, Wash., for the use of Getman's chapter "The Visuomotor Complex in the Acquisition of Learning Skills" in Vol. 1 of the annual series *Learning Disorders*, Jerome Hellmuth, ed.

which he considers an alerting mechanism, the light reflex (i.e., adjusting of the pupil size to light), the grasp reflex, which he feels may be related to attention span, a reciprocal reflex concerned with bilaterality and thrust and counter-thrust mechanisms, the stato-kinetic reflex, which indicates a readiness to act, and a myotatic reflex, a system that provides the muscles with the information that they have acted. These innate response systems are part of the human species design and are found at birth. Getman believes, however, that "the full relationships between different reflexes are established through movement, awareness of movement, and control of movements."

Getman also believes it is important to understand all physiological action systems of the child if we are really going to understand how he learns and that learning is a process of the entire body.

The second level of the model, the *General Motor System,* includes skills of creeping, walking, running, jumping, skipping, and hopping. These activities provide for exploring and extending bilaterality.

The third level, *Special Motor Systems,* includes a new and more elaborate combination of the first two levels or systems. Abilities at this level include eye-hand relationships, combinations of the two hands, hand-foot relationships, voice, and gesture relationships.

The fourth level is that of the *Ocular Motor Systems,* where the matched and balanced movements of both eyes is the main concern. Parts of this system are (1) *fixations,* or the ability to fixate quickly on a target; (2) *saccadics,* or the movement of the eyes from one target to another; (3) *pursuits,* or the following of a moving target; and (4) *rotations,* or the ability to move both eyes in all directions.

Speech Motor Systems is the fifth level of Getman's model. This level includes skills of babbling, imitative speech, and original speech.

The next level is that of *Visualization Systems,* made up of immediate intersystem relationships by which one could, for example, see something from the feel of it. Another example is that of a past-future relationship, which allows for reviewing what occurred yesterday or previewing what will occur tomorrow.

As visualization ability increases, *Perception* or *Vision* can occur. They derive from the operation of all the underlying systems.

Perception, according to the model, could be a single perceptual event or a construct that is "loaded with different but related aspects or components of the informational input."[12] The comparison of the single perceptual event with the construct results in *Cognition*, the next level of the model. Getman said that most learning programs assume the child has reached *Perception* and is moving to the *Cognitive* level.

Above *Cognition*, Getman includes abilities such as analogs and abstractions, imagination, relativity, and expression, which jointly lead to intellectual developments.

In *The Physiology of Readiness*, Getman and his associates* planned practical lessons for developing perception. The six programs are:

1. Practice in General Coordination. The purpose of these exercises is to help the child become well enough coordinated so that he does not have to think about the movement of his body. He is freer, then, to explore the world and to receive information. Some of the exercises are different types of head, arm, and leg movements, rolling exercises, races, crawling, jumping, hopping, and skipping.
2. Practice in Balance. These exercises help the children to explore the relation between the right and left sides of the body, to improve balance, and to direct their movements with their eyes. Various walking exercises on a wooden beam are used.
3. Practice in Eye-Hand Coordination. These exercises relate the visual and motor systems of the child. Drawing circles and lines at the chalkboard in various planned ways make up these exercises.
4. Practice in Eye Movements. These exercises attempt to develop control and accuracy of eye movements. Ocular fixation, span, and sweep are all practiced.
5. Practice in Form Recognition. The development of form perception is necessary before children can learn to read words. Templates are used by the children to draw circles, squares, triangles, rectangles, and diamonds. After drawing them with the template, the children practice drawing free hand, which is the beginning of visual memory training.
6. Practice in Visual Memory (Imagery). To develop visual memory, a tachistoscope is used to project circles, squares, or other shapes

---

* From G. N. Getman, Elmer R. Kane, Marvin R. Halgren and Gordon W. McKee, *The Physiology of Readiness*, 1964. Courtesy P.A.S.S., Inc., Box 1004, Minneapolis, Minn.

on the wall. After seeing each picture, the child must close his eyes for a specified time, then open his eyes and either name the shape, trace it in the air, mark the correct picture on a worksheet, trace over the pattern on the worksheet or draw one from memory. This task increases in difficulty as forms are combined in various and increasingly more complex ways.

Though Getman's views derive chiefly from a consideration of the ocular mechanisms and visual perception, his thinking involves considerably wider areas. The reader will note points of communality between Getman's work and that of Kephart and, especially, Barsch.

A NEURO-PHYSIOLOGICAL APPROACH

Carl Delacato

Two phrases that underlie much of the theory and treatment identified with Delacato* are: (1) "If the problem lies in the nervous system, we must treat the nervous system,"[13] and (2) "Ontogenic development . . . recapitulates the phylogentic process."[14] The rationale that relates these two ideas was best expressed by Delacato himself.[15]

Neurological organization is that physiologically optimum condition which exists uniquely and most completely in man and is the result of a total and uninterrupted ontogenetic neural development. This development recapitulates the phylogenetic neural development of man and begins during the first trimester of gestation and ends at about six and one-half years of age in normal humans. This orderly development in humans progresses vertically through the spinal cord and all other areas of the central nervous system up to the level of the cortex, as it does with all mammals. Man's final and unique developmental progression takes place at the level of the cortex and it is lateral (from left to right or from right to left).

This progression is an interdependent continuum, hence if a high level of development is unfunctioning or incomplete, such as in sleep or as the result of trauma, lower levels become operative and dominant (mid-brain sleep and high cervical pathological reflexes).

---

* From Carl H. Delacato, *The Diagnosis and Treatment of Speech and Reading Problems*, 1963. Courtesy Charles C Thomas, Publisher, Springfield, Ill.

If a lower level is incomplete, all succeeding higher levels are affected both in relation to their height in the central nervous system and in relation to the chronology of their development. Man's only contribution to this organizational schema is that he has added to the vertical progression, the final lateral progression at the level of the cortex. Here again, at the cortical level, the same premises apply. The final progression must become dominant and must supersede all others. Prerequisite, however, to such dominance is the adequate development of all lower levels. In totally developed man the left or the right cortical hemisphere must become dominant, with lower prerequisite requirements met, if his organization is to be complete.

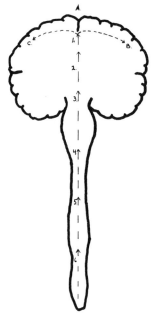

A. The point to which animals slightly lower phylogenetically than man can arrive. B. Point to which totally developed left-sided human arrives. C. Point to which totally developed right-sided human arrives. Numbers denote lower neural levels, which affect higher levels and are in turn affected by higher levels. Upon failure of a higher level, next lower level becomes dominant.

FIGURE 10. NEURO-ORGANIZATIONAL SCHEMA (POSTERIOR VIEW)
(Courtesy Charles C Thomas, Publisher, Springfield, Illinois)

Phylogenetics is the study of the evolution of man. Phylogentically the nervous system has evolved from a very simple to a very complex mechanism. As evolution progressed, animals achieved what could be compared to a spinal cord. These animals operated chiefly at a reflex level. As time went on in the evolutionary cycle, the mid-brain was developed, and finally there evolved animals which operated slightly under the level of man, who has a cortex. Through the evolutionary cycle man has developed a cortex, yet vestigially he retains the lower-level neurological appendages and functions which were needed during this developmental cycle. If the animals which operate slightly under the level of man are analyzed they are found to have a cortex. Generally, they have the neuroanatomical structure of man but these animals cannot do the following things: stand fully upright, see three-dimensionally, oppose the thumb and forefinger, supinate and pronate the hand, speak or write a language, and operate unilaterally with hand, foot and eye of one side of the body.

The neurological differences between man and slightly lower forms of animals are not cellularly important. The basic difference between man and the animal world is that man has achieved cortical dominance wherein one side of the cortex controls the skills in which man outdistances lower forms of animals. This whole phylogenetic process is recapitulated ontogenetically with each human being. In the event that there is some obstruction to this ontogenetic recapitulation, communication and language dysfunctions occur.

Man has evolved to the point that the two hemispheres of the brain, although they mirror each other physically, have differentiated functions. Right-handed humans are one sided, i.e., they are right-eyed, right-footed, and right-handed, with the left cortical hemisphere controlling the organism.

Trauma of the controlling cortical hemisphere results in loss of language skills, but equally important, trauma of the subdominant area results in loss of tonal factors. Left hemiplegics (right-handed people who have suffered a cerebro-vascular accident to the right or subdominant hemisphere of the cortex) have no difficulty with speech but suffer a very significant loss in tonal memory, tonal appreciation, and the ability to carry a tune. Generally, their melody, rhythm and accent abilities are affected.

Some investigators feel that man's supremacy is not the result of cellular acquisitions within the cortex but is instead the result of the specialization of function which man has evolved in the use of his cortex. They feel that as man evolved into an ideating and communicating human being, he simultaneously developed cortical laterality.

Aphasia, delayed speech, stuttering, retarded reading, poor spelling and handwriting, and reading within normal range but below mathematical performance are, in that order, decreasing degrees of the same problem, according to Delacato. These are six symptoms of communication dysfunction, and a child who is successfully treated in one problem will begin to exhibit signs of the succeeding problem. For example, a delayed-speech child could be expected to stutter as he progresses through his communication problem. Underlying all of these symptoms is neurological disorganization, some of which, in Delacato's view, is due to treatment of symptoms rather than the underlying neurological disorganization itself.

According to Delacato, neurological organization proceeds toward the cortex as myelinization of nerves takes place. The progression is regular and predictable. Organization of a lower level is prerequisite to organization at a subsequent level. The subcortex must be organized before the cortex, and hemispheric dominance cannot be established until cortical organization has occurred. This organization begins before birth and normally takes about eight years. At birth, the spinal cord and the medulla are typically the highest organized structures. These structures must function on a largely reflexive basis if life is to be sustained at all. At about four months of age, the child has begun his development toward mobility and leaves a stage characterized by a neural organization at the level of fish and proceeds, through involvement of the Pons, the seat of the tonic neck reflex, to an organization characteristic of amphibians. Audition and ocular-motor functions are involved at this level. This reflex, first evident before birth, tends to cease at about twenty weeks of age. Presumably, cortical organization is responsible for the inhibition of the reflex. The tonic neck reflex has utility not only in the birth process, but in homolateral crawling movements. It is obvious to Delacato that a child in whom the tonic neck reflex is poorly developed or impaired through trauma will have difficulty with subsequent steps of neurological organization. During sleep, the inhibition of the cortex recedes and the vestigial tonic neck reflex again returns. Thus, according to this theory, a well organized child will tend to sleep in a homolateral position (i.e., arm and leg flexed on the same side of the body), with the head turned toward the flexed limbs. Sleep pattern thus becomes an index of the level of neural organization. Ears and eyes are functioning at this level, but the ears do not work together sufficiently to locate sounds in space and similarily, the eyes do not operate in concert.

At about six months of age, neurological organization has reached the level of the midbrain. Again, the functions subtended by this part of the nervous system begin at about this age. To paraphrase Delacato, midbrain functions bring the child from the level of an amphibian to that of a "land animal."[16] Requirements for creeping have been met: binaural audition, binocular vision, and direct relationships between neural fibers associated with sight, sound, balance, posture, and movement. At this stage cross-pattern function (opposite hand and leg) emerges.

Some aspects of the clinical examination are typical of any reading clinic (e.g., handedness, eyedness, and footedness tests, visual function tests, near- and far-point vision) while other aspects are unique to Delacato (e.g., creeping, sleep pattern). Treatment, however, is not typical of that found in other reading clinics. With rare exception, treatment is initiated at the level of neurological organization indicated in the examination. Thus, a child whose organization has reached only the medulla (typically he would be a mobility problem) would be programmed for organization at the next higher level by (a) allowing him the opportunity to use available reflex movements and (b) passively imposing those movements on him if he is incapable of them. Similarily, treatment at any level of organization is aimed at reorganizing subsequent disorganized levels. In training at the level of cortical dominance, procedures are applied simultaneously, for what is being trained, in the words of Delacato, is not "a foot, an eye or a hand, but . . . a hemisphere of the brain. The retraining of one area alone cannot result in the establishment of hemispheric dominance."[17] The first step, at this level, is the deletion of tonality (music, TV sound, etc.). The child will first become more noisy in an attempt to provide his own tonality, but will gradually become quieter. The retraining of sleep patterns is followed by training in footedness, handedness, and finally, writing. However, subcortical organization must be complete before handedness training. The result of training only the hand in attempting to establish cerebral dominance is, according to Delacato, too often the cause of stuttering. Very careful and detailed treatment for eye training is given. A re-examination of the neurological reorganization precedes the actual instruction in reading. On satisfactory achievement of reorganization, instruction in reading commences.

The logic of Delacato is forceful. The learning of tool subjects depends upon a certain level of neurological organization. If the child has not achieved the prerequisite organization because of slow or faulty development, or trauma, such learning cannot occur. The great unspoken assumption of Delacato is that one can succeed in reorganizing the nervous system of such a child by revisiting the operations of childhood in a systematic way. Presumably, an infinity of explanations about the operation of the human nervous system could be generated. Any of them might be correct. It is unlikely that we will arrive at the "whole cloth of truth" in time to apply its fruits to today's handicapped children. Thus, from the practical standpoint, empirical research is indicated. Delacato himself maintains that all techniques of remediation should be subjected to rigid, controlled study, and he contends that results should be the only criteria used to justify any treatment rationale.[18]

LINGUISTIC APPROACHES

Since language defects or lags are often characteristic of children with learning disabilities, it could be expected that certain remedial procedures that put the primary stress on ameliorating language problems (i.e., listening, speaking, reading, writing) would be evolved. It is not the rather widespread prevalence of language problems among children with learning disabilities that justifies this approach, however, since almost all handicapped children have language defects. It is, rather, the positive relationship of language ability to measured intelligence and to school achievement that makes such approaches important for children with learning disabilities. For presumably improvements in language function can lead to improvements in intellectual function and/or academic achievement, and these latter are precisely the areas in which children with learning disabilities need improvement. The nature of these relationships was explored in the chapter on differential diagnosis.

Samuel T. Orton

Orton* in his book *Reading, Writing, and Speech Problems in Children* 'noted that psychological and environmental influences play an important part in language development, but even allowing for these things, there are "inherent or constitutional differences in certain children, apart from those of general intelligence, which markedly influence their acquisition of the language function."[19] It was toward these differences and their satisfactory treatment that Orton's work was directed. Although he died in 1948, his work on laterality and dominance, his descriptions of children's developmental language problems, and the techniques he employed in teaching children still serve as a basis for a great deal of diagnostic and remedial work being done today.

In developing his theories, on which he based treatment, Orton looked to man in earlier ages and noted that man's superiority comes from two things: (1) communication with others of his kind, and (2) manual dexterity. It is interesting, he said, that both of these are controlled in only one of the two cerebral hemispheres.

Man's ability to communicate expressions of emotion begins early in infancy and probably developed early in human history. Animals, he pointed out, can communicate emotional sounds and so can children, even those with marked defects in brain development. Symbolic language, however, is much more complex and is always dependent on training. As in the child, spoken language developed in the human race long before written language. Orton defined symbolic language as "a sign or a series of sounds which has come to serve as a substitute for an object or a concept and can thus be used as a means of transferring ideas."[20] The use of this symbolic language, that is, the language faculty, with which Orton was chiefly concerned, was the capacity to (1) understand the spoken work, (2) reproduce it, (3) understand the written word, and (4) reproduce it.

Orton described the development of an individual's language in stages, beginning with infant babbling. As the motor speech mechanism becomes integrated with the auditory centers, the child begins to echo the vocal sounds of others, without necessarily

---

* From Samuel T. Orton, *Reading, Writing and Speech Problems in Children,* 1937. Copyright renewed 1964 by June L. Orton. By permission of W.W. Norton and Co., Inc.

understanding their meaning. Next comes the association of sounds with the object or idea they represent. As a child's vocabulary increases, he proceeds from the use of nouns to verbs, to sentences, and gradually to longer and more complex language groupings, until, at about the age of six, he is usually ready to acquire a new set of language symbols for reading and writing.

In certain otherwise normal children, however, language development may falter at one or more of these stages. In order to understand these deviations, Orton turned to the study of language losses in brain-damaged adults to find the physiological pattern by which reading and the other language functions are governed. From his own clinical and autopsy work and from the medical literature, Orton selected the following facts as important: (1) The area of damage is more important than the amount of brain tissue destroyed—a small lesion in a critical area can do as much damage as extensive injury elsewhere. This indicated to Orton that malfunction is caused by a disturbance of cerebral physiology rather than a destruction of areas of registration. (2) One brain hemisphere is all-important in the language process and the other either useless or unused. A very small area of damage in a critical area in the dominant brain hemisphere may give rise to a severe loss in speech or reading, while a similar area of destruction in the non-dominant hemisphere will be followed by no language disorder whatsoever.

Orton described three levels of physiological complexity at which brain damage could occur. Using vision as an example, the most severe damage would result in "cortical blindness" in which there is no conscious vision although the eyes themselves are not defective. Damage at the second level could bring about "mind blindness" in which the patient sees objects but is unable to recall their use or purpose. At the third level of damage, "word blindness" could occur, where there is no loss of vision or the ability to interpret pictures or objects; only the printed word no longer has meaning for the patient. In the field of hearing, comparable examples could be given. On the first level, a person could be deaf because of brain damage, on the second level the patient hears sounds but does not interpret them, and on the third level the patient hears and interprets non-language sounds such as a doorbell, but does not understand the spoken word. Orton said that destruction of the appropriate cortical areas in both hemispheres is necessary before level one, and probably before level two, symptoms occur. For level three, however, a lesion in only the dominant hemisphere is sufficient to cause a disorder of spoken or written language.

Orton found parallel symptoms in adults with language losses due to brain injury and in children with developmental language problems and believed, therefore, that a disturbance in the same physiological processes was involved in both instances. Since in the adult a language problem occurs only when damage is in the dominant hemisphere, Orton sought to study those factors that tend to determine the choice and establishment of unilateral brain control in children. He found that many children with language problems were motor intergrades. For example, they might be right-handed and left-eyed or they might perform some skilled acts with the left hand and others with the right. Because of this mixture of right and left motor skills, he reasoned that there could also be comparable intergrading between critical areas of the brain for the various language abilities, thus giving rise to a series of developmental disorders in language. He noted that in the normal adult, handedness, footedness, and eyedness indicate which half of the brain is dominant. Damage to that side can also affect language. Orton assumed, therefore, that in a child "variability could exist in the establishment of the unilateral patterns in language development comparable to the demonstrable variation in the motor pattern."[21] He pointed out, however, that the occurrence of motor intergrading is not a fixed measure of a person's ability to acquire either manual or linguistic skills; many individuals with some degree of mixed-sidedness have experienced no difficulty in learning complex motor acts or spoken or written language.

Orton's study of language problems in children began with reading disability and extended to special writing disability, developmental word deafness, motor speech delay, abnormal clumsiness, childhood stuttering, and combinations of these syndromes. He held that no general formula can be given for the treatment of any one syndrome because each case is an individual problem and a tailored program must be set up for each child. He did, however, find one common trait running through all six problems covered in his book: a difficulty in sequencing or repicturing the exact order of the letters, sounds or other units. This led to his offering the term *strephosymbolia,* meaning "twisted symbols," which describes the difficulty without necessarily implying the existence of a brain defect.

Specific reading disability (developmental alexia) was defined by Orton as the inability to learn to read with the rapidity and skill that would be expected from the individual's mental age and achievements in other subjects. This handicap can be found in all degrees of severity. The child with this problem will be unable to recognize printed words readily. He may confuse reversible letters and words (e.g., *b* and *d*, *was* and *saw*). He can often copy written words but cannot write to dictation without error. Both oral and written spelling are poorly retained. These symptoms will be found in other children, especially beginning readers, but the child with alexia will exhibit them to an oustanding degree. Obviously, in making a diagnosis in cases of reading retardation, possibilities of mental retardation, hearing or vision loss, or emotional problems must also be considered.

Children with specific reading disability may be right- or left-handed, but many cases of this type have crossed patterns of intergrading, i.e., they may be right-handed and left-eyed, or they may do some things with the right hand and some with the left. Also, according to Orton, the majority of such cases have a family history of left-handedness, and often there are language disorders in other members of the family.

Children wih milder cases of specific reading disability will learn to read but usually later and less well than others of the same intelligence and age. As their reading becomes more complex, comprehension may become more difficult. Although they may understand each word, they may still have trouble with longer sentence or paragraph meanings. Spelling ability may be five years behind arithmetic as measured on standard tests. These cases usually do not receive attention until their reading problems begin to block progress completely in high school or college. Learning to read and write a foreign language will be very difficult for them although they may encounter no such difficulty learning to speak it. Their vocabulary remains limited and they never read for pleasure. Hard effort producing little success cannot fail to discourage these children greatly, and they often react with secondary emotional disturbances.

Orton's treatment of specific reading disability began with the smallest language units the children could handle. Because flash cards presenting a whole word at one time left these children very confused, Orton broke the word down, and since they had no trouble with spoken sounds, he began by teaching the phonetic equivalents of printed letters. The sound of a letter was linked to its printed symbol by having the tutor present a card with a single letter, giving the sound, and having the child repeat the sound until he had learned it. For children who reversed letters, the kinesthetic pattern was established at the same time by having the child trace the letter pattern as he gave its sound. After teaching each consonant sound with the different vowels, their proper blending, in the exact sequence in which they occurred in a word, was begun. This was the heart of the problem for children with specific reading disability. When the child could thus say a word aloud, he could understand it because he was already able to understand spoken language. To assist the child in establishing the habit of consistent left-to-right reading, Orton approved of pointing with the finger, using movement as a guide. The associative links, he said, must also be trained for spelling. That is, after teaching the child to give a sound when shown the printed letter, the drill was reversed, having him say and write the letter when the sound was presented to him orally.

As the child progressed, Orton suggested training in oral reading, study of phonetic choices, word families, prefixes and suffixes, simple derivations, and the requirements of grammatical construction. For older children who had learned, with difficulty, many short words but still had trouble with sequencing, he suggested using nonsense syllables and words (telling the students that they were nonsense words) in the drills.

Orton felt that children with these problems should be found as early as possible because some methods of teaching reading (as the whole word method) confuse them and add to their problems. A preventive program designed for their needs would be much more effective in teaching them to read than a remedial program started two or three years later. He pointed out that it may be difficult to detect these children, especially the milder cases, because most children exhibit the same errors when learning to read. Orton suggested watching especially for (1) stutterers whose impediment began with earliest speech, (2) children with difficulty in understanding the spoken word, (3) children who were abnormally clumsy, (4) children who were late in developing handedness, and (5) children with a family history of left-handedness or developmental language disorders.

In summary, Orton's plan when working with children with specific reading disability began with a very "careful analysis of the language function from both the oral and visual standpoint and the institution of measures aimed at the correction of the more patent shortcomings."[22] The program was highly individualized and depended upon tutors with considerable educational background.

Specific writing disability (developmental agraphia), according to Orton, is an unusual difficulty in learning to write. This could coexist with a reading and spelling disability or occur as an isolated developmental disorder. He listed two types, one in which the child wrote satisfactorily but very slowly and another in which the quality of the writing was very poor. Some of the second group also wrote slowly.

The essential aspect in the treatment of special writing disability was an accurate determination of the child's handedness. If there were indications that he should be writing with his left hand, he was shifted on a trial basis. Orton believed that this, again, was a very individual problem and that no absolute rules could be set down. Practicing with the paper properly slanted and determining the child's most natural slant were also important. To train kinesthetic patterns, the child copied from the blackboard while his paper was blocked from his view. In cases showing little progress, Orton suggested that it might be better to teach them typing.

Developmental word deafness is difficulty in learning to understand spoken words, with a consequent delay and distortion of speech. When speech does evolve, the child may become verbose, misusing words and making errors in pronunciation and grammar. Orton found that when young, such children were often overactive, exploring the environment by vision and touch. Because of their poor verbal understanding, they were slow in developing concepts, which could limit their mental development. Minor degrees of word confusions (malapropisms) were frequently found in cases of this disability. Children with developmental word deafness showed the same directional confusions as specific reading disabilities. Most of these children seen by Orton did not seem to have a preferential choice for either hand and most had a family history of some form of language disability or left-handedness.

Orton's treatment of developmental word deafness was based on the assumption that the difficulty in making meaningful associations with the spoken word lay in an inability to recall a sequence of word sounds in their correct time order. Such a child should be taught to say the separate speech units first, and then to blend them into syllables and short words, while at the same time fixing an association with meaning through the use of objects or pictures. To aid in language understanding, only short, simple sentences were spoken to the child. Gradually, these increased in length and complexity. Improvement resulted, in Orton's cases, in ability both to understand the speech of others and to express their own ideas.

Motor speech delay (developmental motor aphasia) was described by Orton as a delay in the development of speech that was not a result of deafness or of defect in the peripheral speech mechanism. Unlike children with developmental word deafness, these children had a good understanding of the spoken word and were not suspected of deafness. Their auditory attention was usually good and they rejected words spoken to them by the examiner with their own defective speech pattern. They were slow in learning to talk and slow in choosing a dominant hand, often showing marked intergrading on motor tests. These children responded well to treatment. In fact, milder cases cleared up spontaneously, with only minor speech defects.

Again, the basic part of Orton's treatment was based on blending sounds in a correct sequence after the individual speech units had been mastered through conventional speech correction methods. First one consonant and one vowel sound were combined; then longer sequences in both words and nonsense syllables were practiced. A phonetic approach to reading was found to be of value in clearing up any residual speech defects after the child entered school.

Many of the children Orton worked with had shown rapid speech improvement at the same time that they began to use one hand or the other as a dominant one. Orton had experimented with training one hand to be dominant but was not sure how much this contributed to their improvement, as they were also having corrective speech work.

Unusual clumsiness in children (developmental apraxia) was defined by Orton as unusual difficulty in learning patterns of skilled movement, sometimes involving movements of the body as a whole as well as manual dexterity. He included this group in his studies because "motor inaptitude" may be a factor in certain types of speech and writing disability and also because an acquired apraxia may result from a unilateral lesion in the dominant brain hemisphere; hence, they seem to belong physiologically with the various language functions. These children are unskillful with either hand, and even with extended training there is usually a close balance between the two hands. They often will be late in learning to walk, run, skate, dance, ride a bicycle, etc., and in using their hands, feeding themselves, dressing themselves, or in playing games or performing other motor activities. Although they may be good at their studies, they are often embarrassed by their clumsiness and withdraw from group activities.

The treatment suggested by Orton was similar to that in the other cases already discussed and was based on teaching the child the simpler units of the faulty motor patterns and then combining them in proper sequence.

Stuttering in childhood was included in Orton's book because of its tie-in with handedness and his feeling that it was caused by failure of one side of the brain to achieve dominance. Orton identified four types of histories for stutterers: (1) those who have been forced to shift from one hand to the other, (2) those who have been slow to select a dominant hand and who show marked intergrading, (3) those with a strong family history of stuttering, and (4) those who seem to have none of the above, but in whose families either language disorders or left-handedness can be found.

The treatment of childhood stutterers depended on the age at which stuttering began. Those who stuttered when they began speaking at age two or three were examined to see if they were using the preferred hand. If they had been taught skills with the non-dominant hand, the other was substituted. If they showed no clear preference for either hand, the right hand was usually encouraged. Speech training was begun on individual sounds, proceeded to blending short units of speech, and gradually moved to longer units and words. If the child was old enough, work was started on connecting spoken sounds with written letters because these children often had reading problems and often, according to Orton, had trouble in joining letters smoothly in writing.

Children who began stuttering later, at about six to eight years of age, were also examined for handedness. If they should have been writing left-handed, this was tried. Sometimes, Orton said, this alone will cure stuttering in this age group. For those who needed more help, sound blending was begun after any defective speech units were corrected. Oral reading was practiced, with the child tracing the initial letter of each word at exactly the same time he started to pronounce it. Gradually he would need to trace fewer and fewer words. Opportunities for reciting memorized speeches were offered, but recitation in school was cut down or eliminated. Other measures adopted were aimed at the prevention of the emotional problems which can complicate the stuttering problem in adults.

Combined or mixed syndromes were mentioned by Orton as cases with complicating factors, which could be analyzed and treated accordingly, although he felt that where a developmental delay occurred in all three pathways to the brain—the visual, the auditory, and the kinesthetic—the prognosis was none too good with the techniques then available.

Orton concluded that, "Many of the delays and defects in the development of the language function may arise from deviation in the process of establishing unilateral brain superiority in individual areas. Such disorders should respond to specific treatment if we become sufficiently keen in our diagnosis and if we prove ourselves clever enough to devise the proper training methods to meet the needs of each particular case."[23]

Barbara Bateman

Bateman* considers a child with learning disabilities to be one revealing a significant discrepancy between what he can do and what he is doing. Moreover, such a child should not be primarily mentally retarded, emotionally disturbed, or visually or auditorily handicapped. Within this framework, her suggested approach to remediation tends to be eclectic and to stress language problems.

Diagnosis, according to Bateman, must be more than classification. It should be "the process of determining which methods are best suited for a given youngster's problems."[24] She views the diagnostic-remedial process in five stages.

Stage One. To begin, it is necessary to determine if a learning disability exists and if it is severe enough to warrant remedial work. How much of a discrepancy between capacity and performance is

---

* Permission granted by Special Child Pub., Inc., 4535 Union Bay Place, N. E., Seattle, Wash., for the use of Bateman's chapter "An Educator's View of a Diagnostic Approach to Learning Disorders" in Vol. I of the annual series *Learning Disorders*, Jerome Hellmuth, ed.

necessary before one should consider it a remedial problem depends on factors such as the age of the child, his health, his present and past rates of growth, and many others. No rigid criteria can be set, but "common sense" should be the prevailing guideline.

Stage Two. If a disability seems to exist, a complete behavioral analysis and description of it is necessary. Besides knowing the level at which the child operates, the clinician now must try to discover how he performs.

Stage Three. Correlates of the disability also must be examined. Bateman identifies two classes of correlates.

1. Para-constitutional factors, which include a "familial factor, sex of the child, 'soft' signs of neurological dysfunction, mixed laterality, motor awkwardness, inter- and intra-test score variability, spatial disorientation, primitive body image, etc."[25]

2. Educational correlates, which include auditory and visual discrimination, sound blending, and many other factors related to academic achievement. Standardized tests are used to find weak areas, which should then be studied in depth. Bateman suggests checking language thoroughly, to see if the child understands what he sees and hears and if he can express ideas with gestures and in speech. She also suggests checking the intermediate processes of language, including assimilation, (which is organizing, categorizing, and generalizing information) storing of language, and retrieval or recall of language.

Studying the correlates of a learning disability helps determine the cause, but the real purpose of the diagnosis is to get information that can be of value in planning a program for the child. This leads to Stage Four.

Stage Four. At this stage, it is necessary to prepare a "clear, concise, and accurate diagnostic hypothesis."[26] Bateman calls this the Janus step, for it points both to everything that has gone before and to what should come ahead.

According to Bateman, a good diagnosis should (1) avoid technical terms, (2) have strong support for any disability indicated, (3) find patterns of related problems, rather than unrelated weaknesses, and (4) recommend remediation.

Stage Five. This stage is concerned primarily with making educational recommendations based upon the diagnostic hypothesis formulated in Stage Four.

To conclude, Bateman's overall plan for working in remedial situations would begin with the five-stage program above followed by the planned corrective work, continual evaluation of the child's progress, and further work based upon the evaluation.

Douglas Wiseman

Wiseman,* more than Bateman, utilizes language for both diagnosis and remediation of children with certain types of learning disabilities. He distinguishes the following key language abilities: auditory and visual decoding, association, memory, automatic auditory or visual closure, and vocal and motor encoding. This terminology derived from his chief assessment device, the Illinois Test of Psycholinguistic Abilities (1961). Remedial exercises are assigned directly from a consideration of the deficit pattern revealed on the ITPA. Exercises suggested for specific deficit areas appear below.

Decoding. These exercises help the child to gather information from the environment and to understand what he sees and hears. Auditory exercises consist of games such as silly questions answered by "Yes", "No", or "Maybe", or a game in which the child looks for a hidden object and is aided by being told he is "hot", "cold", or "warm", along with other clues. Verbal directions can be made into a game (e.g., "Simon Says"). Stories can be told after which the child may be asked to retell parts of the story or answer questions about it. This can be as easy or difficult as the teacher wishes.

Visual exercises include identifying objects in picture dictionaries, catalogues or magazines, identifying colors, letters, numbers, and geometric forms, identifying the meaningful content of an action picture and telling the story of a picture.

Association. Association is defined by Wiseman as the process of "manipulating concepts to form new ideas."[27] Using some facts that a child learns in school in a practical way outside of school is an association process, as is seeing the relationship between two objects.

Auditory association exercises could include classifying objects (naming objects that belong in a house, for instance), building

---

* From Douglas Wiseman, "A Classroom Procedure for Identifying and Remediating Language Problems" in *Mental Retardation,* Vol. III, No. 2, April, 1965. Courtesy of the American Association on Mental Deficiency.

concepts by discussing the way things are alike or different, and asking cause and effect questions, like "What would happen if . . .?"

Visual association exercises include grouping pictures by class (birds, animals, etc.) and finding a picture that is not like the others in a group and explaining how the other pictures have something in common (e.g., truck, car, bike, *boat*). Giving a child pictures, each of which tell part of a story, and having him place them in proper order is another exercise requiring the use of visual association.

Memory. Wiseman lists two types of memory—general memory, which is a global, gross form of retaining information, and sequential memory, which pertains to remembering things in a specified order. There are also degrees of memory. Recognition, the less difficult, requires the child to remember which of several alternatives is correct, while recall demands retrieval responses with few or no clues. In addition, a time element enters into memory, with distinctions drawn among immediate, intermediate, and long-term memory functions.

Some activities suggested by Wiseman to develop the different aspects of auditory memory are: repeating sentences word for word, having the children repeat a story that has been read to them, chanting groups of words and having the child chant them back, chanting groups of numbers or sounds with the children imitating the sequence, and sound blending exercises in which children say sounds separately before attempting to integrate them into a word.

Visual memory (global) tasks include showing the children slides or movies that tell a story, and then talking about it or retelling it after it is over. In a simple task, children look at a page of pictures, and after the pictures are removed, they will try to pick out pictures like those they have just seen. A variation is to have the children tell what they saw on the page. Placing some objects in a certain order, mixing them up, and then having the children arrange them as originally placed, is another game. For older children, a word can be flashed on a screen for a short time, after which the children can try to write the word from memory.

Another idea for sequencing numbers is to help the children learn the phone numbers of friends and relations, and allow them to dial the numbers at the appropriate times.

Automatic Closure. This is described as the "accidental, non-purposeful acquisition of the subtleties of the environment."[28] An example of this is the language patterns children learn (without conscious awareness) in the grammatical structure of a sentence. Children experiencing difficulty in such learning often exhibit errors in time and distance concepts and have difficulty in blending non-meaningful sound elements into a meaningful whole.

One auditory exercise to help develop the automatic process is sound blending. For this, the teacher says the sounds of a word separately, and the child tries to give back the whole word as a single unit. Other exercises suggested by Wiseman include having the child complete a sentence started by the teacher, and teaching pairs of words so that saying one will stimulate saying the other. Developing an awareness of sentence structure is an important closure exercise. The teacher, according to Wiseman, should supply correct models of sentence structure for the child to imitate and, hopefully, to overlearn. He also feels that the child should be encouraged to speak at all times in complete sentences.

Visual closure exercises include having the children name shapes of shadows, ink blots, or cloud forms. Using pictures with partially hidden objects for the children to find helps to develop this process. Completing a form by looking at a finished model, or connecting dots or numbers to make some shape or picture and naming it before it is finished, are additional exercises suggested by Wiseman.

Encoding. Encoding, or expressing, Wiseman said, is the "internal generation and formulation of ideas that may or may not be expressed vocally or motorically. However, the organism is prepared to reply if called on."[29] Vocal exercises include describing an object and telling a story about it, explaining how to do some task, or discussing how to solve some real or hypothetical problem, such as how many ways one could use a pencil, or how the world would change if every one had only one leg.

Motor exercise refers to expressing ideas through gestures or actions. Some of these are the use of pantomines, imitation games, drawing pictures that say something, and playing charades.

The teacher or clinician is not restricted to the above exercises. Indeed, Wiseman encourages teachers to create their own exercises. Once the definition of each ability is understood by the teacher, a number of appropriate exercises can be planned.

The advantage of this approach is its relative simplicity. The defect pattern is immediately discernible from test results and remedial exercises are generated readily. It is, however, based upon the assumption (discussed in the next chapter) that direct treatment of linguistic symptoms can bring about the amelioration, or the reduction, of certain forms of leaning disabilities.

Wiseman holds that most teachers have used similar activities in their classroom work. The key element of a successful remedial language program, however, is the regular and intense application of these activities to the children who need them. He also stresses that not all children with learning disabilities need remedial language training.

DIAGNOSTIC-REMEDIAL APPROACHES IN BASIC SCHOOL SUBJECTS

Grace Fernald

Long before we had a name for them, Fernald* was treating children with learning disabilities in the Clinic School at the University of California, Los Angeles. Fernald approached the remediation of basic school subjects in the spirit of a scientific pedagogist. She once remarked, "All difficulties in individuals of normal or superior intelligence can be removed or compensated for, provided proper techniques can be employed. Emotional disabilities, poor physical adjustments, and difficulties in school subjects can be overcome if proper diagnosis and treatment can be provided."[30]

Whether failure in school is due to emotional problems or vice versa is not clear, but uniformly, practitioners observe that school failure and emotional problems are related. Fernald listed four conditions to help cope with this problem:

1. Do not call attention to emotionally loaded situations.
2. Do not use methods by which the individual cannot learn.
3. Do not subject a child to conditions which cause him to feel conspicuous or embarrassed.
4. Try to direct the child's attention to his progress rather than to what he cannot do.

These edicts, axiomatic now, were insightful in the early days of the UCLA Clinic School.

---

* From Grace M. Fernald, *Remedial Techniques in Basic School Subjects,* 1943. Courtesy McGraw Hill, New York, N.Y.

Fernald's method of teaching reading begins with finding some means by which the student can learn to write words correctly, motivating such writing, and then having the child read a printed copy of his written work. Ultimately, there will be extensive reading of materials other than the child's own compositions.

In the first stage, a word chosen by the child is written or printed in large letters on a card. The child traces the word with his finger, saying each part of it in a natural way as he does so. He repeats this process as often as necessary to learn to write the word from memory. The word card is filed in a large alphabetized box by the child. Next, he should try to use the word in a story. At first, these will be only one sentence. When he has written a story, it should be typed for him as soon as possible, so that he can read it in print. Fernald stressed that it is important that the child trace with his finger and have contact with the paper, that he copy the word without looking at the word card, and that he write the word as a whole unit. If mistakes are made, the process must be begun over, with the child tracing again and then writing on scrap paper without looking. Any incorrectly written or half-finished words should be put out of sight.

The next step is the same as the first, except that tracing is dropped. The child merely looks at and says the word, then proceeds as before. This stage begins when the child is able to learn words without tracing. Usually it drops out gradually, with the child tracing some words and merely looking at others. With this stage, the large file box is replaced by a smaller one and the teacher writes the words in ordinary size.

In the third stage, word cards are not used. The child looks at the printed word, says it, and writes it while saying it. This is the stage where the child begins to want to read from books. He is allowed to read anything he wants and as much as he wants. He is told words he does not know. When he finishes reading, new words are gone over and written by him. Words are checked later for retention.

The next step is concerned with teaching the child to recognize new words from their similarity to words or parts of words he has already learned. Because extensive reading is necessary at this time, Fernald did not read to the children during this stage of remedial work and she asked the parents not to read to the child at home. For difficult materials, the child should glance over a paragraph, underlining words he does not know. As each word is told to him, he can look at it, say it, look away, and write it. After this he should be able to read the paragraph readily.

Work must be continued at this stage until the children can go back to their proper grade and make progress, or for older pupils, until they can read with speed and comprehension any material suited to their intelligence and age.

Fernald believed children should begin reading their own stories first, rather than those adults had written for them. She felt that it was of primary importance that the child's interests and ideas motivate the reading and writing content. She also felt that success was necessary for favorable conditioning to reading and other school subjects, because failure can cause emotional blocking which stops all progress.

Wayne Otto and Richard McMenemy

Otto and McMenemy* offer a pragmatic approach to the problems of children with learning difficulties. Their book, *Corrective and Remedial Teaching*, is addressed to (1) the classroom teacher who will work in special ways with students in her class who are in need of corrective work, and (2) the remedial teacher who will work with children individually or in small groups, probably taking them out of the classroom for the teaching session. Corrective teaching is given "within the framework of regular classwork either to the entire group or to smaller subgroups for the purpose of remedying deficiencies in skill mastery that are interferring with adequate achievement."[31] The second group will consist of children with more severe learning problems, generally considered truly disabled learners.

According to the authors, there usually is no single causal factor in a learning disability, and trying to pinpoint any one cause will be fruitless. Otto and McMenemy use diagnosis primarily to determine what children need help (survey diagnosis) and what skills they need help with (specific diagnosis). Severe learning disabilities may require more thorough diagnosis (intensive) to discover the underlying causes of the problem. The authors do not believe in doing intensive diagnosis unless necessary because, "While it

---

* From Wayne Otto and Richard McMenemy, *Corrective and Remedial Teaching*, 1966. Courtesy Houghton Mifflin Co., Boston, Mass.

is important to seek all the information that will be useful, it is also important to sense the time to stop. Diagnostic information is useful only when it dictates remedial treatment; beyond that it becomes an academic gymnastic."[32]

Diagnosis, according to the authors, must be ongoing during the course of remedial work. A complete diagnosis and remedial program should not be prepared before teaching is begun, but, instead, a tentative diagnosis, prognosis and proposed treatment should be prepared. As the teaching proceeds, necessary modifications can be made in the program.

Some of the key questions to which the authors seek answers from ongoing diagnosis are:

1. Is the child a slow learner or a disabled learner?
2. Will he work best alone or in a group?
3. At what level should the instruction begin?
4. What motivates or interests the child?
5. Where is the child experiencing success?
6. What specialists should be consulted?

The many techniques and materials suggested for use in different teaching situations present a wide variety of viewpoints, which the authors hope will be a useful guidebook for the corrective or remedial teacher.

EPILOGUE

This brief summary of some of the major treatment procedures applied to children with learning disabilities was meant to be exemplary, not comprehensive. Because of the limitations of space, many other useful and widely employed approaches were not discussed (e.g., Monroe, 1932; Bryant, 1964; Harmon, 1965; de Hirsch, 1965; Gillingham and Stillman, 1960). Others (e.g., Haeusserman, 1958; Haring and Phillips, 1962), are discussed under other topic headings elsewhere in this volume. There is no paucity of approaches employed and employable on children with learning disabilities, owing in part to the wide diversity of symptoms and symptom complexes that admit a child to membership in this group.

REFERENCES

1. Later philosophies emphasized the importance of maturation and the use of normal educational approaches at the appropriate time.
2. ALFRED A. STRAUSS and LAURA LEHTINEN, *Psychopathology and Education of the Brain-Injured Child*, (New York: Grune and Stratton, 1947) p. 17.
3. Personal correspondence, printed with permission.
4. STRAUSS and LEHTINEN, *Psychopathology and Education of the Brain-Injured Child*, p. 132.
5. NEWELL C. KEPHART, *The Slow Learner in the Classroom*, (Columbus, Ohio: Charles E. Merrill Books, Inc., 1960) p. 158.
6. RAYMOND BARSCH, *A Movigenic Curriculum*, (Madison, Wis.: Bureau for Handicapped Children, 1965) p. 3.
7. Ibid., pp. 5-6.
8. For reliability and validity data see Maslow, Phyllis, Marianne Frostig, D. Welty Lefever, and John R. B. Whittlesey, "The Marianne Frostig Developmental Test of Visual Perception" in *Perceptual and Motor Skills*, Mono. Supplement II, Vol. 19, 1964, pp. 463-499.
9. G. N. GETMAN, "The Visuomotor Complex in the Acquisition of Learning Skills," in *Learning Disorders*, vol. I, Jerome Hellmuth, ed. (Seattle: Special Child Pub. of the Seattle Seguin School, Inc., 1965) p. 52.
10. Ibid., p. 61.
11. Ibid., p. 63.
12. Ibid., p. 72.
13. CARL H. DELACATO, *The Diagnosis and Treatment of Speech and Reading Problems*, (Springfield, Ill.: Charles C Thomas, Pub., 1963), p. 18.
14. DELACATO, *The Diagnosis and Treatment of Speech and Reading Problems*, p. 77.
15. CARL H. DELACATO, *The Treatment and Prevention of Reading Problems*, (Springfield, Ill.: Charles C Thomas, Pub., 1959), pp. 19-22.
16. DELACATO, *The Diagnosis and Treatment of Speech and Reading Problems*, p. 53.
17. Ibid., p. 122.
18. Personal correspondence.
19. SAMUEL T. ORTON, *Reading, Writing and Speech Problems in Children*, (New York: W. W. Norton and Co., Inc., 1937), p. 19.
20. Ibid., p. 15.

21. Ibid., p. 68.
22. Ibid., p. 178.
23. Ibid., p. 200.
24. BARBARA BATEMAN, "An Educator's View of a Diagnostic Approach to Learning Disorders," in *Learning Disorders,* vol. I, Jerome Hellmuth, ed. (Seattle, Wash.: Special Child Publications of the Seattle Seguin School, Inc., 1965), p. 221.
25. Ibid., p. 228.
26. Ibid., p. 234.
27. DOUGLAS WISEMAN, "A Classroom Procedure for Identifying and Remediating Language Problems," *Mental Retardation,* vol. 3, no. 2, (April 1965), p. 21.
28. Ibid., p. 23.
29. Personal correspondence.
30. GRACE FERNALD, *Remedial Techniques in Basic School Subjects,* (New York: McGraw-Hill, 1943), p. 2.
31. WAYNE OTTO and RICHARD McMENEMY, *Corrective and Remedial Teaching,* (Boston: Houghton Mifflin Co., 1966), p. 38.
32. Ibid., p. 47.

5

THE FIELD TODAY

UNTIL RECENTLY, neither special educators nor regular educators have manifested a particular concern about the child in the twilight zone between normalcy and established handicap. Today this child is being recognized under many titles such as the culturally disadvantaged, the dropout, the educationally retarded, the slow learner, and the child with learning disabilities. Generally found in the regular classes, they are failed, socially promoted, or assigned to remedial and other ancillary specialists. Doubtless, some arrangement could be worked out where, as a matter of routine, regular-class children requiring it could receive work in special classes and vice versa. Except for rare exceptions, such rapprochement has not been achieved and the problem of what to do with these twilight-zone children has persisted.

Recently, however, some solutions have begun to emerge for each type of child. Multi-track programs and ungraded primaries provide for slow learning children; remedial specialists seek to ferret out and correct deficits in the educationally retarded; the culturally disadvantaged children appear to respond to early identification and enrichment. But children with learning disabilities present a special kind of problem. Their deficits do not appear to stem from cultural disadvantagement, low intelligence, or poor teaching directly, but rather from disorientation in those perceptual or conceptual processes required in the learning of school subjects. Techniques that are proving useful with such children derive from two orientations: (1) the process orientation, and (2) the tool subject orientation. The first approach, process orientation, attempts to identify the learning process responsible for the defective performance and apply remediation at this level, hoping for improvement in all tool subjects which rely on the adequate functioning of that learning process. Special educators have been the chief contributors in this area. The latter approach, tool subject orientation, attempts to develop techniques to teach a tool subject (e.g., reading, arithmetic) to children who have failed to learn via methods employed in the regular school class. The modus operandi is to identify the specific areas of poor performance, and apply to these specific remedial measures. Remedial specialists have been the chief contributors in this area.

This chapter, then, is a report on some applications of these techniques, and on the professional activities of the teachers, teacher training institutions, and research laboratories in the field of learning disabilities.

ILLUSTRATIVE CLASSROOM PROGRAMS

When compared with regular classes, classroom programs for children with learning disabilities are distinctive in their materials or methods, or both. Their operation tends to follow the theoretical preferences prevalent in the locale. The program descriptions[1] which follow include a *Visual-Perceptual-Motor Program*, a *Linguistic Program*, and a *Diagnostic Remedial Program*. It is reasonable to expect that, as experience is gained in these programs supporting the efficacy of some methods and denying the efficacy of others, programs will become more eclectic and it will be more and more difficult to characterize classroom programs as representing given theoretical positions.

A Visual-Perceptual-Motor Program

A specific class in a midwestern city has been used to exemplify this program. The materials and methods derive rather directly from the movigenic theory of Barsch. According to the proponents

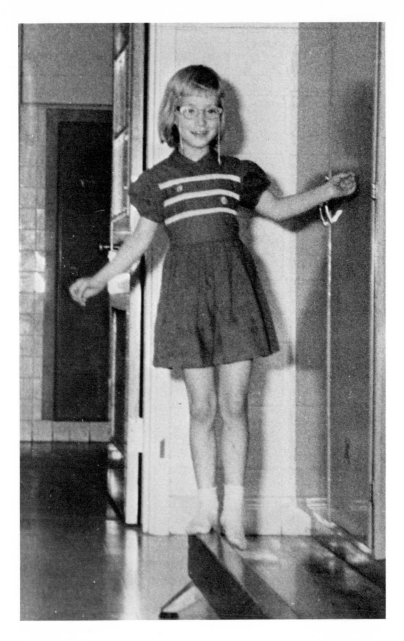

FIGURE 11. Rail-Walking Activity in a Movigenic Classroom

of this general approach, academic learning is dependent upon the prior establishment of perceptual and motoric skills. Accordingly, the materials and methods employed in such classrooms are not academic in the usual sense of the word. Ten children attended this particular class, five in the morning and five in the afternoon. The specific recommendation of the school psychologist was necessary for entrance to the program. These children would have been required to repeat kindergarten had this program not existed.

Appearance of the room. A number of things set this room apart from the regular classroom. Large numerals and geometric shapes were painted on the floor. A walking board, a large inflated inner tube (used as a small scale trampoline), islands of carpet, and various colored paper X's pasted on the wall were among the more atypical features. Other unusual characteristics included window shading and door shading for deliberate light control, portable screens to block off bits of the environment from the child or vice versa, and the absence of fixed furniture. Figure 11 illustrates some of these features.

Some of the more typical equipment found in this classroom includes a piano, tables and chairs, cupboards, chalkboards and pegboards.

Activities. A description of some of the activities will illustrate the use of the equipment and show how materials and methods implement the underlying pedagogical approach.

1. The Walking Rail. Each child was required to walk forward on a 2″ x 4″ board set on edge, keeping his eyes fixed on a target (usually a colored "X" pasted on the wall ahead). If the child experienced difficulty in focusing on the target, an auditory clue (bell) was sometimes given from the vicinity of the target. Children were also required to walk backwards on the board.

2. Patterning Exercises. The children, lying flat on the floor, slid their left knees from a straight to a bent position and their left arms from a side to a raised position while turning their heads left. The same exercise was repeated using the right limbs. See Figure 12.

As the children gained in skill, they practiced turning one part of the body to the right and another to the left. Another exercise required the child to lie at one end of a carpeted area and roll, leading with his head and shoulder, to the right end of the carpet while watching an eye level target ("X"). It was important for the

FIGURE 12. EXAMPLE OF A POSITIONING EXERCISE

child to stay on the carpet and to keep his body straight. Many other patterns were used at different times.

3. Rhythms. Different types of exercises were done in time to a metronome. The children clapped very quietly, raised and lowered their heads until their chins touched their chests, opened and shut their eyes, and bent sideways with arms outstretched. The children took turns choosing or inventing exercises for this part of the program.

4. Reading. Although not part of movigenic theory, each child read aloud his own pack of flash cards. The words were those the children wanted to learn, and some were difficult. The children also read from books written for them using words they knew from the flash cards and written about people and situations with which they were familiar. In addition, a standard beginning reading series was used.

In another reading activity the teacher said a word, and the children would raise their hands high if the initial letter was tall as in "let"; they folded their arms if the initial letter was on the line, as in "see"; and they touched their toes if the initial letter went below the line, as in "pet". If the children needed help, the teacher printed the word on the board.

5. Individual activities. Children also worked alone or with the teacher on activities designed to meet their specific needs. Some of the activities included: games for tactual identification, bow tying, form copying on peg boards, clapping together in imitation, circle drawing, circle and vertical line chalkboard drawing using both hands simultaneously, imitating drum beat patterns, using elastic exercisers, and solving the Montessori peg and hole problems, in which the child must insert the correct size cylinder into the appropriate hole.

6. Visual training. In a darkened room, the children used a flashlight to follow the curved pathways of a large pattern drawn on the board. In other similar exercises, the children followed the teacher's flashlight as she "drew" a line or square or other patterns.

Other more regular school activities, such as rest and snack time, story-telling time, and time for free play, were included in the day's activities.

By relating each of these activities to the positions of Barsch, Kephart, and Frostig in the previous chapter, the reader can discover the underlying intent of each.

In this and other program descriptions, only activities and materials actually seen by the authors are reported. Accordingly, the reader will not get a full appreciation of the overall scope or direction of such programs. But it is clear that in general these programs will aim at returning children with learning disabilities to the regular class, full or part-time, as quickly as possible. Accordingly, all activities, remote from tool subjects as they may seem, will lead to the threshold of the tool subjects as the child begins to overcome his perceptual-motor problems.

A Linguistic Program

In rather vivid contrast to the visual-perceptual-motor program, the linguistic program considers the linguistic problems of the child with learning disabilities as paramount and designs his education accordingly. Patterning exercises, walking boards, and visual targeting are not features of this program.

An experimental laboratory school was chosen as an example of the linguistic program. The methods and materials of this program have been incorporated into the teacher preparation program of the institution sponsoring the laboratory school.

The entrance requirements for this school were more stringent than for the visual-perceptual-motor classes described earlier, though the children admitted were also quite young (CA 3-6 to 7). Each child had at least normal intelligence as indexed by performance tests and exhibited a clear language deficit. Entering children seldom had more than twenty-five words, but they were sufficiently mature to get along in a group.

Appearance of the room. The rooms of this school looked more similar to a regular primary or intermediate classroom than did the visual-perceptual-motor classrooms. A great variety of colorful materials adorned the walls and more furniture occupied the floor space; no attempt at controlling light for instructional purposes was evident. Though the teacher did have a schedule of activities, the structuring and regularity of the visual-perceptual-motor approach was not imposed. Figure 13 shows a primary-level classroom in the school.

Activities. In general, the orientation was to language. The classroom was equipped to stimulate talking, listening, and reading. However, other approaches were employed since not only the traditional aphasic child, but children with reading problems and perceptual-motor impairments were enrolled. Physical education, for example, was provided, with an emphasis on body movements.

A very close relationship with the regular classroom was maintained. Just as soon as possible, the child was returned for all or part of a day to the regular class. Accordingly, irrespective of the problems he presented, as soon as the child showed a readiness for reading, writing or arithmetic, training in these specifics began.

A characteristic of all programs for children with learning disabilities appears to be the close relationship of the school to the parents. In the linguistic program, as exemplified here, parents came for semi-annual conferences, semi-annual classroom observations, and monthly seminars on topics such as brain damage, language development, reading, testing, and legal problems.

Specific classroom activities were such as to demand that the child constantly develop his language ability and practice what ability he had. The stress was much more on ears and mouth and

FIGURE 13. A PRIMARY LEVEL CLASSROOM IN A LINGUISTIC PROGRAM

much less on eyes and movement than in the visual-perceptual-motor classrooms. Toy phones, doll houses, and conversation pieces of all sorts were found in class. Stress was placed on exposing the children to many experiences and then helping them to verbalize these experiences. A great variety of word games was used. Some of the standard techniques of teaching the auditorially impaired and the speech handicapped were employed.

A Diagnostic Remedial Program

For some, the logic of eclecticism, coupled with an awareness that there are differing degrees of severity among children's learning disabilities, has led to a diversification of services, whereby the intensity of the service can be related to the severity of the problem. Children with less severe disabilities can be maintained in a regular classroom if the teacher can be given sufficient help in matching the teaching program to the learning patterns of the child. Children with more severe problems can still be integrated into a regular classroom for a major portion of the day if the teaching in the disabled areas is taken over by a resource or itinerant specialist. Only the most severely disabled may need to be in the special class for the greater part of the day. The concept of more than one type of service for children with learning disabilities takes into account the complex nature of the problem. The program description following was evolved for a midwestern school district. It is characterized by the coordinated involvement of a broad assortment of educational specialists working to meet the problems of learning disabilities to the greatest extent possible within the boundaries of the regular classroom.

The core of this program is a Psycho-Educational Diagnostic Center for Children with Severe Learning Disorders. Personnel involved with the Center include the director, school psychologists, psycho-educational diagnosticians, resource room teachers, classroom teachers who have children in the program, and other special personnel such as speech correctionists, physical education teachers, school nurses, and school social workers.

General plan. Through a screening process, children in the district were selected for intensive individual tests. When this testing indicated that a child had a severe learning disability, the psycho-educational diagnostician or itinerant learning disabilities

FIGURE 14. A Conference-Type Room in a
Diagnostic Remedial Program

teacher began working with the child. This work was done out of the child's classroom but in his own school, usually in a small conference-type room like the one in Fig. 14.

When an effective approach to teaching the child had been evolved, a program that could be carried on in the classroom was mapped out with the classroom teacher. The child's work sessions with the psycho-educational diagnostician were stopped, but the diagnostician remained available as a consultant, program planner, and materials resource person for the teacher.

For children with more severe problems, a resource room program was begun. Under this plan the children still were assigned to regular classrooms, but were taken out during certain periods each day for more specific work. The resource room teacher remained in the children's school all day, working with about ten children whose schedules could be arranged flexibly, according to their needs. For instance, some children came to the resource room more than once a day. Also, if a child reached a crisis situation in his classroom, he could be sent to the resource room where control might be regained more easily. The resource room teacher, with only one school to serve, could give her students more help than a psycho-educational diagnostician could, since she served two or three schools.

Resource rooms, though they seem ideal, have had some problems in actual operation. First, children for a resource room usually must be gathered from more than one elementary school. This requires busing them to the resource-room school with all the attendant difficulties. Second, while the child has a "clean slate" in his new school (and this may be an advantage if he was a disturbance in his old school) he might also encounter problems in making a new adjustment. He may lose old friends and have to make new ones; he will be far from the interests and activities of his neighborhood and he might find it difficult, after school and during vacations, to establish himself as part of the neighborhood. Third, the teachers in a school with a resource room bear a greater burden in the amount of responsibility for these sometimes difficult children than do the teachers in schools from which the children have been taken. Too great a burden could jeopardize continued cooperation and support for the program.

A still more intensive program is the self-contained classroom, where the child is a member of a special class but will integrate

with other classes whenever possible. Only children who cannot
be provided for in the regular itinerant or resource room programs
are assigned here. This is a small proportion of the total of children
with learning disabilities: probably less than 1% of the total school
population.

An interesting aspect of the overall plan is the developmental
first grade. Under this plan, children who otherwise might be
retained in kindergarten are put into a developmental first grade.
Class enrollment is limited to fifteen, and the teacher is trained
in many of the techniques used with children who have learning
problems. Some of the children in this group will go into a regular
first grade, some will go into second grade, some into classes for
the retarded, and some into the program for children with learning
disabilities. This attempt at early identification in order to overcome,
minimize, and/or prevent further learning problems is exemplary
and, we hope, will appear in more school programs.

Approaches. Techniques, methods, and materials used for
teaching by all the diagnosticians and teachers in this program
included remediation exercises based on patterns of disability
revealed by an extensive battery of diagnostic instruments. Remedial exercises were drawn from test patterns on the Illinois Test of
Psycholinguistic Abilities (1961), the Frostig Program for Training
Visual Perception (1964), the Peabody Language Development
Kits (1966), Continental Press materials (1958), sensory-motor
training exercises developed by Painter (1966) and Kephart (1960),
and materials for specialized approaches to the teaching of reading
and arithmetic such as the Initial Teaching Alphabet (1965) or
methods described by Fernald (1943) and Gillingham (1960).
Some of the advantages of this type of program should be noted.

1. Previous work with such children in this school district had been
   limited to the valiant efforts of teachers without specialized help,
   or to private or university clinics, where very few children were
   served. Only through a widespread public school program will
   an appreciable number of children who need help be reached.
2. Shortages of all types of teachers exist, but in areas of special
   education the problem is much worse. If these children are to
   be taught, the regular classroom teacher must do it because no
   one else is available. Her efforts will be successful if specific
   direct help is available to her, and if materials and methods that
   she can use in the classroom are available.

3. Teachers with the possible qualifications for psycho-educational diagnosticians can be found among the personnel presently employed by most school systems. Superior teachers who have taught for a number of years and who have done Master's degree work in individual diagnosis and remediation of learning problems or severe reading disabilities can successfully handle the work. If necessary, teachers who seem to have the necessary training and personality for the work can be encouraged to take additional university course work to qualify for the positions.

4. A program of this type allows for helping children who differ greatly in the severity of their problems. In some cases a child's school performance may be improved with only an adequate diagnosis and short-term remediation, while in other cases constant and prolonged work by the diagnostician may be necessary before the child begins to learn.

This program description embodies the individual remedial approach as a part of a much wider overall scheme, which touches on problems such as the inadequate supply of professional personnel, and the gamut of children with learning disabilities, many of which would be overlooked in a plan which concentrated its resources exclusively on the more severe learning disabilities. We will wish to refer back to this plan in discussing teacher preparation later in this chapter. For the present, the program description of this district was intended to exemplify a more or less "custom-tailored" approach to learning disabilities in which the remediation settled upon is that which produces academic advance.

Summary. While these illustrative programs by no means exhaust the variety of approaches to educating children with learning disabilities, they do exemplify some of the major directions of classroom practice. An immediate reaction to seeing programs "side-by-side" is a realization of the striking contrasts among the programs. On the surface, there are substantial differences.

It is quite possible, as the field evolves, that the heterogeneity of children with learning disabilities can no longer be accommodated by a single term. Children whose major learning problems are perceptual-motor would be helped most by educational programs stemming from that orientation to learning disabilities. Similarly, children whose major manifestation of learning disabilities is in the linguistic area would appear to benefit most from programs oriented in that direction, and so on. Matching child to program orientation is a strategy that is technically feasible today, though it does raise tactical problems for the smaller school systems, which cannot support learning disabilities classes representing a variety of orientations. In such cases, educational planning would simply have to extend beyond the borders of educational units in a manner similar to arrangements now made for the deaf and blind. An itinerant team approach could be regarded as a variation on this theme.

In the long run, it may be possible to prepare specialists in learning disabilities who are sufficiently expert in all the major orientations to accommodate the diversity of symptoms now subsumed under this label.

Clark and Richards (1968) conducted a national questionnaire survey, obtaining a 93% response from the fifty states and three territories to which inquiries were sent. Of those responding, 13 states reported having classes for children with learning disabilities. This, the investigators estimated, represents about 600 programs in the nation. If the present prevalence estimates of learning disabilities are even close to accurate (five to ten percent of the school age population), then one must conclude that only a minute portion of those children requiring special provisions are receiving them.

The problem of bringing order to an already over-diversified field and supplying trained professional practitioners in adequate numbers seems almost overwhelming. Yet the growth of this field in the recent past, the enthusiastic parental participation, the dedicated professional efforts, and the legislative and fiscal support of the federal government are a powerful combination. All these forces are evident in the field of learning disabilities.

TEACHER PREPARATION

To a large extent the nature and supply of teachers for children with learning disabilities will be determined by the institutions that prepare these specialists. Considering the wide assortment of definitions and the variety of educational procedures associated with the field of learning disabilities, it is not surprising that the programs for preparing teachers are something less than uniform. No virtue, of course, attaches to national program uniformity unless all concerned are agreed upon the standards of excellence to be achieved through training, and the amount of virtuosity necessary for practitioners to meet the specific local needs. Such is not the case with the area of learning disabilities. Here the lack of uniformity springs basically from a lack of professional consensus. But high variability is the benchmark of any new field of endeavor and may be encouraged as long as this diversity provides substance to nourish the field's development.

The exact number of colleges and universities offering course sequences leading to certification as a teacher of children with learning disabilities is not known. Chalfant and Kass (1967) reported on eleven such programs, which received financial aid from the federal government as a spur to growth. It is likely that the actual number of such programs exceeds the number funded by a factor of two or three.

Chalfant and Kass reported that all eleven funded programs were graduate programs, the Master's degree and certification being awarded simultaneously. There seemed to be a consensus that the usual 120-hour bachelor's degree curriculum does not provide sufficient time for the student to acquire an adequate level of competence. It is apparent that a prolonged period of preparation for teachers in this area will only aggravate further the present acute shortage of such specialists. Moreover, estimates of training time are based upon expectations that (a) the definition of learning disabilities will not change, and (b) college programs cannot be made sufficiently effective to compress their content over time. One can argue cogently on both of these counts. As long as learning disabilities can mean all things to all people, even six or seven years of training may not suffice to prepare a teacher who can handle all the kinds of problems that may come to her. As the professional field becomes more specific in regard to the definition of learning disabilities, teacher preparation programs can become more circumscribed. Nor is it sure that a Master's degree is necessary for such teachers. It has not been demonstrated that either years in school or number of degrees increases one's success in teaching children with learning disabilities. What is acquired during training, not how long training takes, is the critical variable. Moreover, the need for increasing numbers of competent professionals in special education seems incompatible with an increase in the duration of the preparation period.

Accordingly, uniform adherence to a five-year program of preparation for teachers of children with learning disabilities would seem neither wise nor useful until (a) those who prepare these teachers have achieved some consensus in the definitional status of the term *learning disabilities,* and (b) all reasonable approaches to improving course programming and course density in the colleges and universities have been exhausted.

Present curricula, according to Chalfant and Kass, contain a common core of courses taken by all those preparing to teach children with learning disabilities. These include courses in (a) educational assessment, (b) remedial procedures, and (c) practicum. A wide diversity is possible, and probable, even within this common core. In practicum, for example, imagine the types of experience a student would receive in a program with a perceptual-motor orientation as contrasted with those received by a student in a program with a linguistic orientation. These experiences would be almost as dissimilar as practica for students preparing to teach mentally retarded children are from practica for students preparing to teach the deaf and hard-of-hearing. While the extent and diversity of practicum experience required of any potential special educator varies among and within teacher training institutions, nowhere is the range of variation greater than in programs for teachers of children with learning disabilities. By analogy, wide differences can be expected in the type of training students will receive in educational assessment and remediation. What one assesses and attempts to remediate clearly will affect the nature and extent of the assessment and remediation. In short, this "common core" of training is probably more apparent than real.

A wide selection of electives is generally available to the teacher candidate in this area, ranging from statistics to phonetics, audiology and counseling. Some universities are now providing a sixth year of training for "diagnostic teachers" and a seventh year (doctoral level) for researchers, college teachers, and other leadership personnel in the area of learning disabilities.

It seems fair to conclude that programs for the preparation of teachers of children with learning disabilities are characterized by their diversity. The abilities of the institutional staffs influence not only the quality of the teachers but their orientations as well. As we have seen, these orientations vary widely. It is not likely that we will see "conversions"; proponents of a given view seldom change their orientation. More likely, programs of preparation will become more eclectic, exposing the student to a variety of orientations but preparing them in one. It seems improbable that a student could be prepared for competency in all of the five or six major orientations in the field of learning disabilities, even if the acute shortage of teachers did not preclude the additional training time that would require. The diversity of orientation we have seen is not purely a function of the newness of the field of learning disabilities. A certain amount of diversity seems necessary and we shall probably be contending with the problems it creates for many years.

Teacher preparation programs in general may be affected by predictable administrative changes. Assuming that not all children with learning disabilities have to be educated in a self-contained classroom admits the possibility of flexible scheduling between regular and special educators, between schools, and between school systems. It admits the possibility of itinerant specialty teams to assist regular educators with the less handicapped of these children. It makes more likely a range of treatment intensities, from the self-contained special classroom to minimum assistance of the regular teacher by the special educator. Such changes would require a rapprochment among and within teacher training institutions that does not presently exist.

Chalfant and Kass conclude that research may offer another avenue for solving problems in this area. Applied research efforts can be directed not only to improving the teacher preparation programs but the classroom programs as well. In the following section, this possibility will be explored in greater detail.

EDUCATIONAL RESEARCH IN LEARNING DISABILITIES

Since only a small portion of the research literature could be covered within the limited space allotted to this topic, we have attempted to select studies that represent the range of work being done by today's researchers. Even then it is not possible to provide either complete detail or specific criticism of the studies reviewed. Consideration was given to the selection of studies that are reported in reasonably accessible sources so that the interested reader can consult original studies with relative ease.

The time span of the studies discussed is the early 1960's to the present. The review is arranged under the following headings: Historical Background, Learning Studies, Clinical Diagnosis, Classroom Research, and Educational Procedures. Those desiring more comprehensive research reviews will find them in Edington and Clements (1967), Bateman (1966), or de Hirsch, Jansky and Langford (1965).

Historical Background

The history of research on the educational problems of children with learning disabilities begins with A. A. Strauss and his co-workers. Strauss evolved the idea that retardates fall into two major groups, differing in behavioral symptomatology: the endogenous (familial) retardates, and the exogenous (brain-injured or organic) retardates. His clinical observations led Strauss to the view that exogenous retardates were distractible, hyperactive, emotionally labile. They were thought to possess certain perceptual, conceptual and behavioral deficits, which rendered them in need of educational measures over and above those required for the familial retardate. That the source of these disorders was organic was inferred from the behavioral similarity of exogenous retardates and persons with known brain damage. Exogenous children behaved, for example, much like Goldstein's (1942) brain-injured soldiers.

For methods of testing and teaching exogenous retardates, Strauss drew heavily upon his background in Gestalt psychology. And just as special educators were attracted to his educational methods, researchers were attracted to his claims. For if these claims could be substantiated in the laboratory, a generalized breakthrough would be achieved. Not only would a most important pedagogical distinction have been discovered (replete with methodology) but the findings promised to extend to exogenous children with average and above-average intelligence.

Strauss and his co-workers were themselves responsible for a substantial contribution to the scientific literature, publishing case studies, test development, and specific bits of research substantiating their views (e.g., Werner and Strauss, 1939; Werner, 1944; Werner and Strauss, 1945; Werner and Strauss, 1941; Werner and Bowers, 1941; Werner and Thuma, 1942a; Werner and Thuma, 1942b; Strauss and Werner, 1942a; Werner, 1946a; Werner, 1946b; Strauss and Werner, 1942b; Strauss and Werner, 1943; Strauss, 1944; Strauss and Kephart, 1940; Werner, 1945; Strauss and Kephart, 1939; Kephart and Strauss, 1940).

The legacy of Strauss and his co-workers was the concept of the exogenous (brain-injured or organic) retardate who, among other things, learned differently from his endogenous counterpart and displayed clinically observable symptoms of his organic damage. This theory was to dominate research efforts in the area for almost two decades after the publication of Strauss and Lehtinen's classic text, *Psychopathology and Education of the Brain-Injured Child.*

Learning Studies

One critical test of the Straussian theory would be the actual demonstration that brain-injured children do, indeed, learn differently from non-brain-injured children.

Barnett, Ellis and Pryer (1960) exemplify the type of research which keyed off the work of Strauss and Lehtinen. Noting that special educational procedures were recommended for children with brain-injury, the authors questioned the existence of substantive learning differences between brain-injured and non-brain-injured children in the following way. They matched exogenous and endogenous retardates by sex, age, and so forth, and compared the performance of the groups on tests of:

1. Visual discrimination (selecting a different shape from among three objects, two of which were similar)
2. Mirror Drawing
3. Rotary Pursuit (like trying to hold the tip of a screw driver on a given spot on a phonograph record as it revolves)
4. Double Alternation (learning two alternating patterns of key pressing on an eleven-key apparatus)
5. Finger Maze Learning
6. Serial Verbal Learning (memorizing a ten-word list)

Even when the more seriously brain-injured children were removed from the comparison, the remaining brain-injured children performed less well, as a group, than did the non-brain-injured children on double alternation and serial learning tasks. No differences between the groups were found on the four remaining tasks. The authors concluded, ". . . any general assumption that organics (brain-injured) do not learn as readily as familials, or that they *necessarily* require differential teaching methods, must be qualified."[2]

Subsequent research has tended to substantiate the view that unqualified statements about the brain-injured, as a group, are likely to be in error.

Levine, Spivak and Fernald (1962) found differences in visual discrimination ability between groups of brain-injured, emotionally disturbed, and normal children, favoring the emotionally disturbed and normal children. The findings of this carefully executed study suggested that, in a very basic area of learning, brain-injured children were deficient. The variance in findings on visual discrimination between the Barnett, Ellis, and Pryer study and that of Levine, Spivak and Fernald, could be due to differences in the visual discrimination tasks employed in each study, differences in comparison groups employed, or both. The apparent differences in research findings typifies dozens of such differences that could be found among competent researchers. It illustrates the genuine need for care and caution in interpreting and generalizing research findings on brain-injured children.

Research on the symptomatology of brain-injured children is typified by the work of Cruse (1961), who compared brain-injured and familial retardates for distractibility. Both groups of children were given a reaction-time task during which balloons (anchored and free floating) were blown about the testing room by an electric fan. If the balloons were distracting, and if the brain-injured children were more susceptible to distraction, their reaction time should exceed that of the non-brain-injured familial children. However, no differences were found between the groups, except for the more obviously brain-injured children. This study makes more comprehensible the findings of Rost (1967) and Cruickshank, et al., (1961). In both of these classroom studies of brain-injured children, isolation booths were used to reduce distraction (and presumably distractibility) and thereby increase achievement. Over a period of at least one semester, use of these booths seemed to have little effect for either Rost, or Cruickshank and his co-workers.

Even though the studies reviewed seem to question distractibility as a reliable symptom of brain-injury, extenuating factors such as age, test task, distracting agent, research sampling, and so forth, may be shown, in subsequent research, to be qualifying factors. It is also distinctly possible that all brain-injured children do not display this symptom. Thus, the same caution in research interpretation required elsewhere is required here.

Hawkins and Baumeister (1964) conducted an ingenious experiment, which suggested that the effect of brain-injury on retention (memory) could well be a function of when, and under what circumstances, the brain injury occurred. Forty-two rats were assigned to one experimental and three control groups of 16, 10, 8, and 8 rats, respectively. All groups were trained on a simultaneous black-white brightness discrimination task (T1). Then, the experimental group (E) and the first control group (C1) were trained on a second task (T2), a successive black-white brightness discrimination task. Within a day following the completion of this training, the rats in the E group and the second control group (C2) were systematically brain-injured through operative procedures. Sham operations (surgery with no brain-injury) were performed on the C1 group. The third control group (C3) was surgically brain injured only after all work was accomplished with groups E, C1 and C2, thereby permitting in the C3 group a period of delay after learning, but before brain-injury. The table below reviews this procedure.

TABLE 1

RESEARCH DESIGN FOR THE HAWKINS AND BAUMEISTER EXPERIMENT

Group	Order of Learning Tasks		Surgery	Relearning Tasks
E	T1	T2	Brain-injured	T1
C1	T1	T2	Sham Operation	T1
C2	T1	—	Brain-injured	T1
C3	T1	—	Delay Brain-injured	T1

After a seven-day recovery period from surgery, all rats were retrained on the simultaneous black-white brightness discrimination task (T1) and groups were compared with each other on the basis of the number of retraining trials it took to bring the rats back to their pre-operative performance levels. The performance of Group E was significantly poorer than that of the control groups (Group E did not "remember" as well). Thus, interpolating a different but somewhat similar learning task (T2) between original learning (T1) and brain injury seemed to impair retention. Interpolated learning alone (C1), brain injury alone (C2), or the mere passage of time before brain injury (C3) did not markedly affect relearning. The authors concluded that the effects of brain injury on retention must take into account the learning history of the organism.

To the degree that one can generalize from the situation of highly controlled laboratory animals to the highly uncontrolled and more complex human child, these findings suggest that the fact of brain injury is not sufficient information from which to deduce learning characteristics in those children whose brain damage did not exist from birth.

Clinical Diagnosis

The constancy, or lack of it, of symptoms of brain injury affects not only learning, but the very diagnostic-clinical evaluation processes by which such children are identified and assigned to remedial learning situations. Accordingly, clinicians as well as laboratory researchers have shown an interest in this area of research. Schulman, Kaspar and Throne (1965), in a book-length treatise, exemplify the attempt of clinical researchers to investigate the link between symptoms and brain injury.

The authors hoped to determine whether the techniques commonly used in diagnosing brain-injured children were accurate, whether behavioral attributes thought to be common to brain-injured children (e.g., distractibility and hyperactivity) were consistently detected, and whether measures used to diagnose such children could be used to predict behaviors supposedly common to these children.

Using clinical and case study methods, the authors attempted to classify, sort, and process information in a manner that answered their questions. The diagnostic tests administered by the authors permitted two broad approaches to diagnosis: the *functional discrepancies* approach and the *cumulative signs* approach. In the former, differences between performances on two tests or between two sections of a single test were sought. It was reasoned that wide discrepancies could be regarded as an indicator of brain injury. In the latter approach, clinicians sought the types of behavior (signs) alleged to be associated with brain injury in children. These signs were totaled in the hope that when they were sufficiently numerous, a diagnosis of brain injury might be indicated.

Findings were essentially negative. According to tests commonly used to diagnose children with brain injury, their subjects could not be regarded as brain injured. It was clear, however, from the authors' description of their subjects that these children did, in fact, possess abnormalities of the central nervous system. Moreover, subjects did not exhibit a brain-damage syndrome; that is, no common set of "signs" was found that would characterize a child as brain injured. Finally, with some exceptions, the child's behavior could not be predicted from the results of diagnostic tests.

Some specific findings from this major work deserve special mention. In studying hyperactivity, the authors found that the situation largely determined the amount of activity and that the total activity of their subjects was within normal limits. In fact, in a structured situation, their subjects were less active than expected. The authors attempted to explain this rather unusual finding by noting that: (1) their subjects were growing into adolescence and might be losing some of their "driven" behavior at this age, or (2) brain injury might create activity deviations both above and below normal levels, or (3) these children were selectively less active than other children with brain damage. Others (e.g., Schranger, 1966) have found hyperactivity to be one of the more consistent symptoms of brain injury.

The authors found a small but positive correlation between distractibility (the inability to "maintain concentration on a desired set of stimuli in a variety of situations",[3]) and brain injury. Emotional lability, defined as the instability of subject behavior in the face of relatively unchanging stimulus configurations, was found to correlate moderately with brain injury.

The diagnostic approaches employed by the authors are in fairly common usage. They suggest that the functional discrepancies approach be used cautiously and only as an indicator of the need for further testing. The use of discrepancies between scores on sections of a single test is particularily suspect, because these sections tend to lack sufficient reliability. Problems associated with the cumulative signs approach to diagnosis were: (1) the authors found that no single test could differentiate among all forms of brain-injury, and (2) circularity may have been involved in their methodology, since subjects with known brain injury were used as the criterion for deciding which tests and items signified brain injury.

Schulman, Kaspar, and Throne concluded that ". . . brain damage appears to be very complex with consequences that vary according to both the extent and locus of damage."[4] Since the same symptoms may appear with dysfunctions other than brain damage, "the diagnosis of brain damage should be used sparingly and made only when a large number of diagnostic indicators agree."[4]

Classroom Research

Not all research data have come from the laboratory or clinic. Increasingly, the classroom is being involved in research in an attempt to produce findings that have immediate practical value for the educational practitioner. Such work is exemplified in a study by Haring and Phillips (1962). This research is available in book form, and though it was said to have been done on emotionally disturbed children, these children seemed to be the kind whose affective problems stemmed from neurological impairments. The authors described their subjects as having good mental ability but unable to integrate and direct their efforts toward realistic educational goals, as having neuromuscular coordination problems that interfered with learning, and as having good vision and hearing but experiencing trouble in translating what they saw and heard into meaningful action. Their behavior was unpredictable, erratic, uncontrolled and hyperactive.

Forty-five such children, at the fifth grade age level or lower, were divided into three groups for a year, and were pre-tested and post-tested on achievement and appropriateness of behavior. Group I received a highly structured organized program in which a definite schedule was followed. Directions were brief and clear, assignments were individualized, isolation booths were provided, and the completion of assignments was expected. Group II was dispersed among six regular classrooms where the teacher and ancillary staff worked out and executed special programs that accorded with each child's interests and abilities and permitted success and recognition. Punitive responses to a child's aggressive or rebellious behavior were avoided. Group III was assigned to a permissive classroom where the curriculum was modified to suit the interests of the child and where a warm, friendly teacher allowed the children to express their feelings and anxieties. Limits were avoided where possible and, in the main, an attempt was made to meet the real emotional needs of the child.

After the first year, Group I children had gained almost two years in achievement, going from a second grade to a fourth grade level of achievement. Group II gained a year. Group III gained about .7 of a year. A behavior rating scale supported the view that Group I children had achieved significantly more in this area as well.

Though one may find some design problems in this study, it is significant because it was carried on for a full year in actual class-rooms, using a reasonably large sample of children. It tends to support, for children with characteristics similar to those which have come to be identified with learning disabilities, the value of a highly structured classroom situation and individualized educational programs.

To summarize, the symptoms of brain injury suggested by Strauss and his co-workers appear to be elusive and inconsistent when scrutinized by researchers in the laboratory, clinic, and classroom. Indeed, by the early 1960's, the usefulness of utilizing the concept of brain injury in educational planning had been called openly into question. The significant problem for educators was not the fact of brain injury; it was, instead, the presence of certain behaviors in the child's repertoire, which made learning difficult or impossible. It was such observations that were ultimately responsible for the shift in labeling from *brain injury* to *learning disabilities*.

Educational Procedures

Some research has been reported on all of the educational procedures reviewed in Chapter 4. Such research has been exemplified, in the present review, by selected studies bearing on the efficacy of procedures that stress the linguistic, perceptual-motor, and neurological disturbance aspects of learning disabilities.

Linguistic Disturbances. With professional stress on Straussian symptoms of brain injury, linguistic defects received relatively little attention. Though difficulties of speaking and understanding speech were alluded to by Strauss, no elaborate testing and treatment apparatus was supplied for such problems as had been provided for tool subjects such as reading and arithmetic. But studies in the field of speech and hearing and in the medical literature had long since associated linguistic impairment with brain injury (e.g., aphasia, dyslexia). The diagnostic value of linguistic defects, in the field of learning disabilities, had also received increasing recognition over the years. Scherer (1961), for example, attempted to predict achievement in brain-injured children and found that only the Binet, a highly verbal test, had any useful predictive value. In a similar vein, Haring and Ridgeway (1967), in attempting to assemble a battery of tests which could be used to identify children with learning disabilities, found (as had their predecessors) that while no single instrument was adequate for the task, language ability was the best single index.

Thus, though the existence of linguistic handicaps in individuals with neurological impairment has been noted since the 1800's, the relationship of this observation to children with learning disabilities is of recent origin. The utility of linguistic performance in diagnostics and as an index for remediation has been enhanced somewhat by the apearance of test batteries such as the PLS (Parsons Language Sample, Spradlin, 1963) and the ITPA (Illinois Test of Psycholinguistic Abilities, Kirk and McCarthy, 1961). These tests, which purport to measure different linguistic abilities, promised to yield the functional discrepancies that Schulman, Kaspar, and Throne had sought, and the success-failure patterns that could distinguish children with learning disabilities from numerous other handicaps, in which linguistic impairment is also a symptom.

The ITPA has been used in studies involving the mentally retarded, the gifted, the visually handicapped, the auditorily impaired, the culturally deprived, the speech handicapped, children with low IQ's, and neurological impairments such as cerebral-palsied and aphasic children. Olson (1961) compared the performance of sensory-aphasic, expressive-aphasic and deaf children on the ITPA and found some consistent differences between the first and last of these groups. Expressive aphasics were too variable in their individual performances to yield any basis for prediction. In a similar study of aphasics and hard-of-hearing children, Reichstein (1963) found the latter significantly superior on all but two of the nine ITPA subtests. The two subtests on which the deaf and hard-of-hearing were not superior measured visual and motor performance. Myers (1963) attempted to distinguish two types of cerebral-palsied children, spastics and athetoids, on the basis of ITPA performance. Such children represent clearly brain-damaged individuals whose motor impairment testifies in some degree to the differential site of the cerebral lesions. Under such circumstances, differential linguistic performance might be expected. Discriminant analysis of the data suggested that the groups did differ in performance, as predicted.

Collectively, these studies suggest that (a) children with brain-damage do less well linguistically than those without such damage, and (b) there may be some linguistic symptom differences that could be used as a basis for remedial planning. The ITPA has also been used for studying the child with reading problems (Bateman, 1963; Kass, 1963; Ragland, 1964; McLeod, 1967). These studies all suggested that the abilities measured by the "non-meaningful" part of the ITPA are defective in these children. This is somewhat contrary to the popular notion that reading is a highly "meaningful" process. Kass, for example, used the ITPA and a number of additional tests with dyslexic children. She found the greatest deficit areas to be indexed by tests like sound blending, mazes, memory for designs, and perceptual speed. Kirk (1968) suggested that learning disabilities are of three varieties—academic disorders, nonsymbolic disorders, and symbolic disorders. Reading problems represent an academic disorder but could actually stem from a nonsymbolic (non-meaningful) disorder. The research cited above suggests that this may indeed be true. In this framework, the ITPA can be viewed as one general tool for distinguishing between symbolic and nonsymbolic disorders associated with some types of learning disabilities.

Just exactly how problems in acquiring and using language relate to learning disabilities is not clear. However, basic linguistic processes surely underlie the more advanced linguistic processes (e.g., reading, writing). This is similar to Kirk's notion. Another possible explanation derives from the view that learning itself is dependent upon mastery of linguistic skills. Accordingly, linguistic handicaps would lead to learning handicaps. Elsewhere, (McCarthy, 1964) evidence is presented showing a consistent and substantial correlation between the ITPA and the Binet for normal children and several types of handicapped children. The suggestion is made that this relationship between language and intellectual ability may be causal. Thus, if an increase in linguistic ability could be effected, a corresponding increase in intellectual ability would appear. Of course, this is speculative and requires experimental research to confirm. But it is intriguing and could be relevant to the area of learning disabilities.

Other linguistic approaches to learning disabilities have been utilized and predate the psychometric approach characterized by tests like the ITPA and PLS. The work of Myklebust dominates this area. In the general realm of language pathology, Myklebust has long been associated with the classic linguistic disturbances (e.g., aphasia, dyslexia, agraphia) and has published extensively (1954, 1964, 1965). Many years of extensive and intensive case studies have formed and refined his views on language pathology. His approach to learning disabilities is characterized in the Johnson and Myklebust book on that topic, *Learning Disabilities*.

Perceptual-Motor Disturbances. Strauss had concentrated on attempting to overcome the multitude of problems that the brain-damaged child presented to the educator, including perceptual-motor disturbance. It waited upon men like Kephart and Barsch, however, to develop and elaborate distinctive theories about the source of these problems and about their educational treatment. In essence, such theories indicate that the perceptual and motor systems are intimately linked in humans and both relate to higher intellectual functions. Disturbance in either of the systems or in their proper relationships will not only be manifested by perceptual and/or motor performance problems, but can interfere with higher learning processes. Accordingly, remediation would be aimed at ameliorating problems associated with disturbed perceptual and/or motor performance. This would open higher learning processes to appropriate educational treatment. Though oversimplified, this has seemed to be the essence of such theories, and a certain amount of research has related to them.

McCormick, Schnobrick, and Footlik (1966) randomly assigned 32 boys and 32 girls (normal beginning first graders) to experimental and control groups and pretested them on IQ and reading achievement to ascertain initial equality. The experimental children were given perceptual-motor exercises for an hour a day, two days a week for nine weeks. The control group received an equivalent amount of physical education activities. Otherwise, both groups received the regular school program. Post-testing revealed no significant differences between groups. However, from the beginning, the authors had identified a sub-sample of underachievers who had scored below reading level on pre-testing. There were 12 of these in the experimental group and 12 in the control group. Their pretest means in reading were essentially equal. Following the treatment, the experimental group of underachievers was significantly ahead. The study's authors contend that the usefulness of the procedures was demonstrated because the underachieving children, for whom these procedures were designed, appeared to profit. The authors acknowledged the problems associated with their small sample and other aspects of design. Moreover, only a careful examination of the details of their perceptual-motor training program would reveal how closely their operational definition of such training matched the prescriptions of the theorists in this area.

Capobianco (1967) investigated the relationship of reading ability to ocular-motor laterality in children diagnosed as having learning disabilities. Orton (1937) had suggested that incomplete (or non-established) dominance contributed to confusion, which resulted in a variety of learning problems that would, presumably, be manifested in learning to read. A long history of research on this matter has been inconclusive. It was Capobianco's contention that studies on clinic samples supported Orton while studies on non-clinic samples had not. Using subjects enrolled in public school classes but attending a reading clinic one hour daily, the investigator divided the children into two groups, EST and NEST. The former, by their performance on a series of handedness and eyedness tests, demonstrated that they had established both a hand preference and an eye preference, though not all established hand preferences were on the same side as established eye preferences. Such preferences had not been established by the NEST group whose eye and/or hand preferences were variable on tests. Two reading tests were administered to both groups. In essence, the only difference between the groups favored the NEST group, which surprisingly completed its reading tasks in significantly less time than the EST group. Capobianco noted the similarity of this sample's performance to that of a group of mental retardates he had studied previously, in a similar manner. He concluded that laterality preference as part of a diagnostic workup, in a clinic or not, appeared to be of dubious value.

These are but two of a large body of studies that bear on the relationship between theories involving perceptual-motor mechanisms and manifest problems of learning. Though outcomes of this body of research are best regarded as inconclusive, we cannot conclude that the theories are incorrect or the research badly done.

Scientifically, a lack of research consensus indicates inconclusiveness. No implications are permitted.

Neurological Disturbances. Delacato is perhaps the chief proponent of the view that if the nervous system is damaged or dysfunctional, the appropriate educational procedures must begin with remedial exercises designed for appropriate neurological reorganization. This view, too, is being subjected to research scrutiny, with inconclusive results.

Kershner (1968), for example, compared two groups of trainable mental retardates, one which received Doman-Delacato procedures for 74 consecutive teaching days (experimental N = 14) and one which received a program designed to achieve better balance, rhythm, coordination, and body image (control N = 16). Attempts were made to control program content, examiner bias, Hawthorne Effect, and intercommunication between the experimental and control teachers. Children were pretested and post-tested on the Peabody Picture Vocabulary Test (PPVT), creeping and crawling evaluations, and the Kershner, Dusewize, Kershner adaptation of the Vineland Oseretsky Test (VOT) of motor development. Initial equality between the groups was established for age, years in special education, percent of absence, creeping and crawling evaluation scores, and VOT scores. In PPVT scores, the control group significantly exceeded the experimental group. Post-testing revealed no difference on the VOT, chiefly because both groups had improved considerably in motor development. The post-test creeping and crawling evaluations significantly favored the experimental group. The post-test PPVT scores were similar but when they were statistically adjusted for the initial inequality, the experimental subjects were significantly favored. In absolute IQ points on the PPVT, the experimental group had gained about 12 points on the average and the control group had lost about four. The author concluded that creeping and crawling were improved through special exercises, that the recapitulation of early perceptual motor experiences may not be prerequisite, as Delacato suggests, to the development of more sophisticated perceptual-motor skills, and that the PPVT superiority of the experimental group must be accepted with caution because of the statistical and sampling limitations involved. Despite the appropriate cautions of the investigator, these results tend, in part, to support Delacato's approach.

A less supportive study aimed at testing Delacato's theory was reported by Robbins (1966). He selected three nearby classes of "normal" Catholic, Caucasian, lower-middle-class children, who matched reasonably well on age, intelligence, creeping and laterality. Small initial group differences in reading (.3 year) and arithmetic (.4 year) were later equated statistically. Group I (N = 43) was a control group, which continued its normal classroom operation. Group II (N = 38), the experimental group, received Delacato exercises in creeping and crawling, avoidance of music, specified writing positions, sideness and cross-pattern activities, homolateral patterning, and color filtration. The third group (N = 45) was called a non-specific group. It engaged in activities, some of which were contrary to Delacato's suggestions. After three months of treatment, Robbins found no post-test differences among the groups in reading or arithmetic nor did he find the effects of lateralization or creeping beneficial to tool subjects. The investigator acknowledges that there are limitations to his study such as a lack of random selection of subjects and possible differential teaching ability among the teachers, but concludes that his results do not support the theory.

Summary

If there is one word that characterizes the research that bears on learning disabilities, it is "inconclusive." There is sufficient substance to the claims of theorists to lure the researcher into the laboratory, but rarely does his research either unequivocally support or rule out the claims he investigates.

We have seen that the effect of brain injury on learning performance is complex and that factors such as age, onset of brain injury and previous learning history will qualify these effects. The symptoms of brain injury and their diagnostic validity have been called into question in recent research. The use of these symptoms in diagnosis and remediation requires caution and judgment. Broad generalizations connecting symptoms with brain damage appear to be unwarranted. The development of linguistic, perceptual-motor, neurologic and other remedial approaches to children with learning disabilities provides the special educator with a wide array of special techniques. However, behavioral research has not unequivocally supported any of these approaches; certainly, research recommends no single approach to the exclusion of others.

Thus, few generalizations are warranted from the present

research literature on learning disabilities. It appears, however, that the demonstration of cerebral dysfunction or brain injury is of little relevance to the educator. The identification of specific learning problems and of techniques to ameliorate these problems is the major concern. It is unlikely that any single approach to the education of children with learning disabilities will succeed in all cases. The research literature suggests otherwise, for each child presents a different set of learning problems. The best educational approach would seem to lie in using those techniques shown to be successful with each type of problem. Penn's (1966) review of the literature on reading disabilities indicated clearly the feasibility of overcoming learning problems (the inferred origin of which is organic) with appropriate remedial procedures. To create and test such procedures would seem to be a major research goal.

REFERENCES

1. The authors are grateful for the generous cooperation of the school systems visited. Specific mention of the people involved has been given in the Acknowledgments.
2. CHARLES D. BARNETT, NORMAN R. ELLIS, and MARGARET PRYER, "Learning in Familial and Brain-Injured Defectives," *American Journal of Mental Deficiency*, vol. 64, no. 5 (March 1960) p. 899.
3. JEROME L. SCHULMAN, JOSEPH KASPAR, and FRANCES M. THRONE, *Brain Damage and Behavior*, (Springfield, Ill.: Charles C Thomas Co., 1965) p. 97.
4. Ibid., p. 83.

6

PARENT GROUPS

and LEGISLATION

IT IS NOT BY COINCIDENCE that parent groups and legislation are discussed in the same chapter. Since World War II, parents of handicapped children have on their own initiative formed groups that have become very influential in affecting state and federal legislation on behalf of handicapped children. Motivated understandably by concern for their own children, these groups have worked tirelessly and effectively for educational provisions. The outcome of their efforts has been the passage and implementation of laws providing for the handicapped, with benefits extending well beyond the children of parents in these groups. Moreover, their efforts have helped to effect a profound change in the public attitude toward the handicapped.

PARENT GROUPS

Parent groups have emerged as a powerful force for setting the future directions of special education activities. Of course American education has always had the unique quality of local control and hence a susceptibility to the demands of those directly financing it. So, in a sense, parental activity is more a modern revival of increased community concern than a new development. Parents are exercising a prerogative they have always had. Yet in many ways parents of handicapped children have different concerns, concerns which relate more directly to the educational processes and less to overall educational goals, more to pointing to unmet needs to be filled by professional efforts than to supplying directions for filling those needs. Historians will probably regard this movement as enlightened and beneficial, but there is no doubt about the influence of these groups on legislation affecting special education. Clark and Richards (1968), in their recent national survey of programs for children with learning disabilities, found that over half (53%) of the states reported that parental pressure was the basic impetus for beginning programs. No study of special education today is complete without some consideration of the role of parents in the development and implementation of special programs.

Parents of cerebral palsied children were among the first to form groups; then, in turn followed parents of mentally retarded children, emotionally disturbed children, and children with learning disabilities. One can speculate on the powerful motivations that bring parents to such great efforts. It is not surprising that parents of cerebral palsied children were among the first to form large and influential groups to promote an awareness of their children's needs. This is a dramatic and often encompassing handicap. Half the cerebral palsied are mentally retarded, about 70 percent have speech problems, many have associated visual and/or auditory handicaps, and all have brain damage and motoric problems. In a sense, the character of the handicaps motivating the formation of subsequent parent groups has been less dramatic. Thus, retardation is less dramatic than cerebral palsy, emotional disturbance is less dramatic than mental retardation, and learning disabilities are less dramatic than emotional disturbance.

The parents of children with learning disabilities suffer a frustration not usually associated with the more dramatic handicaps. For want of a better phrase, we can call it the "taste of honey" phenomenon. In many of the emotionally disturbed, and in all of the children with learning disabilities, intelligence is essentially normal. The contrast of the normal and subnormal abilities within each of these children seems to create a constant irritation for the parent because in many ways the child does behave normally, which only makes one long all the more for that educational, medical, or psychiatric treatment which can push the child to complete normalcy. Having tasted the "honey" of normalcy in their children, they understandably yearn for more. This inevitably leads to a certain amount of frustration, which is not experienced by parents of children with more devastating handicaps who are not offered this promise. These latter, of course, experience great psychological problems in adjusting to the handicap of their child but they are spared a certain ambivalence, for not having tasted "honey," they can not long for it. These observations may not apply to all parents, for the emotions of parents of handicapped children are individual and complex and best known only by those who have experienced them. But this is clear: the well springs of motivation to act in behalf of their children are very powerful in the parents of the handicapped. The parent-group formations of recent years have been a constructive social reaction to handicap, and beneficial, also, from the standpoint of the emotional health of the parents. One can only guess at the private agony experienced by parents of handicapped children in earlier years when public attitude did not condone the exposure of these children, much less support efforts to optimize the child's potential through education, medicine and research.

The character and extent of present parental involvement in special education is of recent origin. Parents have always been concerned, of course, with the education of their handicapped child. But until perhaps the 1940's, the prevailing attitude was one of secrecy about the child. This attitude was premised on the public non-acceptance of handicaps and fueled by parents' unreasonable feelings of guilt and shame. Kept within the confines of the home, the child was permitted as little public exposure as possible and regarded as a private and personal problem. Cruickshank and Johnson (1958) speculated that the shift in public acceptance of handicaps evolved from the public's tolerance of war-injured adults which spread gradually to include a tolerance of handicapped children. This was, in retrospect, a predictable response from a basically benevolent society. But whatever the historical and sociological roots, a sharp change in the attitudes of parents of handicapped children following World War II is a historical fact. Though the first groups met to discover the solace that comes from knowing one is not alone with his problem, it was not long before courses of action were set down, formal group structures established, memberships sought, and goals clearly established.

The aims of parents, professional educators, and legislators in behalf of handicapped children largely coincide, though often the motivations differ. Occasionally professional educators and/or legislators may disagree with parents on priorities or on means to goals. Major discord, however, seems increasingly unlikely as professional educators and/or legislators identify with parent groups, and as society in general and special education in particular adjust to this vital and massive new force.

In the field of learning disabilities, the scope and speed of the formation and growth of parent groups have been spectacular. California, Illinois, Louisiana, New Jersey, New York, and Texas were among the first states to organize in behalf of such children. New York's Association for Brain Injured Children, and Illinois' Fund for Perceptually Handicapped Children were organized in 1957. The California Association for Neurologically Handicapped Children originally incorporated in 1960 (and reorganized in 1963) grew to twenty-nine state chapters and a paid membership of about 3,000 persons in 1967. By 1967 a national organization, the Association for Children with Learning Disabilities (ACLD), had affiliates in 15 states and Canada and contained about 200 local groups. Its advisory board includes widely known and respected special educators. The parent group movement has been, politically speaking, a "grass roots" movement. State organizations typically result from the affiliation of local groups with common interests. Incorporation as non-profit organizations is usually sought under the laws of the respective states.

Added to the intense motivation of parents of children with learning disabilities was the efficiency gained from utilizing the experience of previous parent groups in their own state, and national organizational and operational methods. Such observations illuminate but do not fully explain the amazing growth of the parent groups. Growth patterns are similar in most of these groups, for the ultimate objectives are the same in principle. Interest in newsletters and resource materials gradually evolves into concern with legislation and national affiliation. National affiliation opens the door to national conventions, the systematic fixing of state and national legislative goals, the production of educational and public affairs materials such as pamphlets, films, and TV spots. Ultimately, concern turns to research and professional education problems. An example of this pattern is the development of the California Association for Neurologically Handicapped Children (CANHC), the large California parents' group. Highlights of its history include:

Spring 1959:   Parent groups organized in Los Angeles and Orange County.

October 1960:   Corporate papers for CANHC filed.
                 Parents appeared before state senate fact-finding committee on special education to describe the neurologically handicapped child, and needed educational programs.

February 1961:   Assembly Bill 3129 introduced (Rees and Unruh) providing educational programs for neurologically handicapped children.

May 1961:   First general meeting of CANHC held.
                 CANHC began publication of the pamphlet *Neurologically Handicapped Child.*

June 1961:   Assembly Bill 3129 failed to pass in senate.

1962-1963:   Sponsors of Assembly Bill 3129 and Senate Bill 616, which provided educational programs for the emotionally handicapped, joined in support of a bill to provide educational needs for "Educationally Handicapped" children (Assembly Bill 464).

                 In May 1963, by-laws were written, a president elected (R. O.'Reilly, M.D.), and the following chapters chartered: Los Angeles, San Diego, Orange, Santa Clara, San Mateo, Contra Costa.

July 1963:   Assembly Bill 464 passed the legislature and was signed by Governor Brown.
                 First CANHC Award-of-the-Year was given.

1963-1964:   This period saw the distribution of public education materials, the beginning of TV programs on the subject of neurologically handicapped children, and the addition of the following chapters to CANHC: Stockton-San Joaquin, Alameda, Marin, Stanislaus, Sacramento, Tuolumne, Bakersfield-Kern, Pomona Valley, Long Beach, and Livermore-Amador Valley.

November 1965:   CANHC movie format was approved for "Why Billie Can't Learn."

September 1965: "CANHC and the NH Child" written by R. O'Reilly was published in a state educational journal.

January 1966:   CANHC-Waldie Scholarship was established in honor of Assemblyman J. Waldie for his contributions to the education of the neurologically handicapped child.

This brief and incomplete review illustrates the growth patterns described previously. In the case of CANHC, the historical record of professional involvement is just beginning to be written, through their awarding of scholarships and their support of national legislation providing for professional training and research in behalf of handicapped children.

It is too early to determine the precise impact of parent groups on special education generally, and in the area of learning disabilities specifically. But it is clear that parent groups have helped to create a positive public attitude toward handicaps in children; they have had a decided effect on the nature and quantity of legislation passed in behalf of the education of handicapped children at the state and federal levels; and they have had a galvanizing effect on professional special educators. The membership of these groups has become increasingly altruistic. Certainly, future parents of handicapped children will be in a better position to educate their offspring as a result of the efforts of parent groups, past and present. As the children of these parents grow older, concern may turn to "non-educational" aspects of living, such as social adjustment and vocational placement, especially if the given handicap persists to adulthood. Beyond this, what future directions parent groups will take is speculative, but such groups can exert a sizable influence in special education generally, and in the special field of learning disabilities.

SPECIAL EDUCATION LEGISLATION

The purpose of the following section is to consider some of the recent legislation that has a direct effect on the education of handicapped children, including those with learning disabilities. Since this legislation is better understood in historical perspective, a brief review of the development of public education[1] in the United States follows.

In all civilized countries today, education is either a governmental function, is intimately related to governmental function, or both. Accordingly, laws and the government (i.e., the people who create, interpret, and execute the laws) are intimately related to the education enterprise.

In the United States, the government unit in closest association with education is the local educational agency. Though the organization, operation, and selection of the members of these local educational agencies vary greatly from place to place, American education (if one can assimilate such a heterogeneous operation into a single phrase) is characterized by the locally controlled, free, public school. This derives from our history.

Historical Background

As early as 1642, the governing forces of the Massachusetts Bay Company, recognizing the need for each of its members to be able to read and understand religion and the capital laws, declared that each of its towns should select men who would implement this requirement. In several of these towns, historical precedent was set when a free school was built and funds collected for the annual salary of the schoolmaster.

By the time the Federal Constitution was adopted, the precedent for local control in education was established and the power to control the education of its own youth was reserved, at least implicitly, to the separate states. From then until now, this has been the pattern.

Each state, via constitutional and statutory enactment, specifies the powers of the local education agencies. Each local educational agency, in turn, enforces those powers specified, powers implied from those specified, and whatever other powers are required to implement the specified powers. Since the responsibility for education is reserved to the states, the federal government cannot act so as to offend in this regard. Though it may influence the states by withholding federal aid-to-education funds until a state has met certain minimum federal standards, it is unthinkable that the federal government would usurp the states' power in educational matters. Some think this uniquely American pattern of education has contributed to the national greatness.

Thus, from the founding of this country, the federal government has been reluctant to interfere with local prerogatives in education. Indeed, it was not until 1867 that a federal Office of Education was established. Even then it was limited to collecting information and promoting the cause of education. The Office of Education was first absorbed into the Department of Interior in 1869, and in 1939 it became a part of the Federal Security Agency. In 1953 the present Department of Health, Education and Welfare was created by a federal reorganization plan in which all the components of the Federal Security Agency were transferred to this new department. The authority of the Office of Education has increased accordingly. Its stated purposes now include the collection and dissemination of information, financial assistance, and special studies and programs. Though the states are still legally independent of the will of the federal government in educational matters, they defy this will at the risk of being denied access to federal funds and assistance. Even the novice historian will recognize some degree of erosion of local autonomy. However, the check and balance relationship between and among the judicial, executive and legislative branches would seem to prevent excessive encroachment upon the rights of the states in education. Moreover, the administrative style of the Office of Education has historically reflected a reluctance to infringe on educational powers reserved to the states.

Legislation

The background of the relationship of government and special education is relatively brief and includes no direct reference to learning disabilities. Special classes were established in some of the larger cities, beginning about 1900, using teachers who had been trained largely in residential institutions. In time, colleges and universities began to assume the training of special educators. At the state level, certification standards were created and a plan was evolved that encouraged local school systems to establish educational provisions for the handicapped through the use of excess cost formulas. Though specifics vary, the concept is the same. The state provides a per child, per classroom, or per teacher unit cost for the handicapped, over and above what it provides for the nonhandicapped. This is based upon the observation that special education, as we know it today, almost universally demands a lower teacher-pupil ratio and hence costs more. Although there is an increase in the budgets of the State Departments of Education, these are offset by savings in the State Departments of Public Welfare, for it is less expensive to educate a handicapped child in a day school class than it is to care for him in a residential institution. By 1930, a majority of the states had some provisions for the education of handicapped children; today, all do.

By 1930, the federal government had established a Section on Exceptional Children and Youth in the United States Office of Education. This unit remained a Section until 1963, when, in implementing certain educational provisions of Public Law 88-164, the Section achieved the status of a Division. Though the Division performed with unusual effectiveness in implementing the new law, it was abolished in 1965 in a reorganization of the U.S. Office. Its personnel and authorities were redistributed. Arguing that such dispersion of functions and personnel could only impede and weaken federal programs for the handicapped, educational leaders such as S. A. Kirk urged the reassembly of these functions at a Bureau level. And, in 1967, under PL 84-750, a Bureau of Education for the Handicapped was created, containing, in turn, three divisions: Research, Educational Services, and Training Programs. The number and types of Divisons in the new Bureau were governed largely by the programs established through laws passed beginning with the Eighty-Fifth Congress.

Over a period of time, there has been somewhat less reluctance on the part of the federal government to authorize programs that affect the educational and special educational programs. The attempt, of course, is not to usurp power, but to improve education. To date this has been done with sufficient tact so that the states, far from rejecting federal aid, approve it and seek it. The concept of federal aid to education appears to be widely accepted today; the problem appears to be whether this should be in the form of general or categorical aids. In categorical aids, the use for the funds is specified; in general aids, it is not. Categorical aid can be conditionally granted, as in cases where *de jure* segregation had to be eliminated before federal funds would be granted. Those who argue for categorical aid see it as a means for raising minimums in education. General aid would involve the distribution of federal education funds on some formula basis, reserving to the respective states the educational purposes to which the funds would be put. Those who argue for general aid to education see the Constitutional intent more fully achieved in it. Moreover, they contend that individual state needs differ and states must have the freedom to apply funds in the areas of their greatest perceived need.

Special educators tend to favor categorical aids. Arriving only recently on the educational scene, and representing a distinct minority, special educational programs cannot always attract needed support. Accordingly, it is felt that if funds are categorically specified for special education, they will find their way directly to the service of handicapped children. If federal aids are general, the established needs of regular education could siphon off much-needed funds. This is especially true with today's burgeoning school-age population and the emphasis on increasing the quality of all education. Present trends favor categorical aid, in fact, categorical aid in which funds are earmarked. Earmarking funds for the mentally retarded, for example, assures that these monies are spent on the education of that type of handicapped child. The obvious benefits of earmarking are somewhat offset by its exclusivity. Funds for the mentally retarded cannot usually be spent for the deaf or for children with learning disabilities. Accordingly, categorical aid earmarked by type of handicapping condition is typically based upon a law which has a "wastebasket" category into which handicaps not included in the primary categories can fall.

This "wastebasket" class is usually a minor form of general aid for a categorical purpose and those who would draw from it must compete as in competing for general aid. A relatively new area such as learning disabilities would be included in such a "wastebasket" category. It is not difficult to understand why those interested in these children prefer to have their category of handicap specifically mentioned in legislation. They could then compete for funds on an equal basis with specifically named categories. This is precisely the aim of parent groups that seek federal recognition of learning disabilities as a category of handicap, though the diversity of conditions now collectively regarded as learning disabilities detracts from the logic of their case. The fact may be, however, that established kinds of handicap (e.g., mental retardation, emotional disturbance) may have only historical justification and, on examination, may also be so educationally heterogeneous as to merit no more recognition as a category than learning disabilities.

Some professionals suggest that the logical problem raised in regarding learning disabilities as a category warrants a much needed rethinking of the manner in which we now group handicapped children for education. Indeed, the door has been opened for considering the wisdom of reintegrating special education into regular education and vice versa. Federal aid to special education accelerates the demand for a resolution of issues such as these.

Though the appropriations associated with Public Law 85-926 were only one million dollars, a precedent was set for larger sums and broader purposes on behalf of handicapped children. Public Law 85-926 provided to colleges, universities, and state educational agencies funds whereby graduate fellowships could be awarded to qualified individuals wishing to prepare for a career in the education of retarded children. Since few teacher preparation programs in mental retardation were at a graduate level, the funds were spent largely to develop badly needed leadership personnel who, as it turned out, were to direct many of the teacher preparation programs in special education, which were established largely through the availability of funds from subsequent Public Laws.

In 1961, Public Law 87-276 authorized funds specifically for the preparation of teachers of the deaf. These funds, made available over a three-year period to colleges and universities, were not restricted to graduate students. These two Public Laws, 85-926 and 87-2761, set the stage for the most spectacular legislation that had ever been passed by the federal government in behalf of the education of handicapped children, Public Law 88-164. In 1963, Public Law 85-926 was amended (PL 88-164) to provide stipends and dependency allowances for persons preparing for careers in special education, specifically teachers, supervisors, speech correctionists, specialists, and administrators in the areas of mental retardation, serious emotional disturbance, speech and hearing impairment, deafness, visual handicap, crippling, and other health impairments (Title III). For each selected student, the college or university would receive a $2,500 support grant. In addition, colleges or universities interested in establishing or expanding personnel preparation programs in special education could apply for a program development grant for that purpose. With this incentive to institutions and students alike, a meteoric rise occurred in the number of personnel being prepared for special education careers. State Education Agencies were given funds, after their state plans for spending them were approved, on a population-based formula. These funds were to be used for fellowships, training institutes, and in other creative ways to strengthen special education in the respective states.

In 1965, the well known Elementary and Secondary Education Act (ESEA), Public Law 89-10, was passed, providing direct educational aid to states. Although handicapped children could be interpreted as included in the massive provisions of this act, there was not a specific category for them. By 1966, however, sufficient strength had been garnered to pass legislation authorizing federal funds specifically for handicapped children. The Morse-Carey amendment to Public Law 89-10 (89-750) became its Title VI. Among its various provisions was the granting of direct aid to programs for handicapped children, awarded to states on a formula basis. Thus, by 1968, two Public Laws, 88-164, Title III and as amended 89-750, Title VI, provided federal funds to educational institutions for training personnel in special education, financial assistance to those being trained, and direct aid to states for their special education programs. And federal funds continued and expanded in the area of research with a new emphasis on application and innovation.

Beyond this, there were numerous additional Public Laws which provided funds, some of which could be legitimately expended upon the special education enterprise. A partial list includes:

P.L. 85-864 National Defense Education Act, Titles III and VII
P.L. 85-905 Captioned Films for the Deaf
P.L. 87-415 Manpower Development and Training Act
P.L. 88-269 Public Library and Construction Act, Titles IV(A) and IV(B)
P.L. 89-329 Higher Education Act, Titles V(B) and V(C)

The authority for these and other acts administered by the Office of Education, suggests the enormous increase beyond the original role of the Office.[2] Student financial assistance, program assistance to colleges and universities, direct aid to states, construction funds for libraries, community health centers, research facilities, adult education, teacher corps, and funds for instructional materials were among the diverse activities funded by the Office. Hardly a Congress since the eighty-fifth has failed to pass legislation that benefitted handicapped children. While no legislation has been passed which specifically earmarked funds for children with learning disabilities, bills have been written which specifically designate such children and it is probably only a matter of time until parents and professionals persuade a beneficent Office of Education of the merits of their case. Already a National Advisory Committee on Handicapped Children to the Office of Education has proposed a

definition which suggests the kind of handicapped child for which
funds may be appropriated and earmarked. (See Chapter 7.)

Government in the United States is responsive to the will of the
governed. It has been, in the last analysis, a revision of public
attitude that has occasioned the spectacular legislative benefits for
handicapped children. Education is still a local prerogative and
the federal government will seek its direction from the governed.
The power of professionals and parents associated with special
education should be exercised with wisdom. There is always the
danger that competition for federal funds will compromise judgment. For example, special education professionals for years have
been questioning the value of the classical etiological categories
(e.g., mental retardation, emotional disturbance) in special education. They maintain that educational communalities should be
established on the basis of similar learning problems, regardless of
what caused those problems. Yet largely for fiscal reasons, the
federal government is encouraged to retain and expand those very
categories in its legislation. And since this legislation provides not
only direct aid to handicapped children and to students in special
education, but to the very institutions which prepare our future
administrators, supervisors, teachers and researchers, it is difficult
to devise and implement a suitable alternative. It is clear that to
obtain federal funds, state education agencies, colleges, and universities must apply for funds within categories and be prepared to
defend their expenditures within these categories. In all of this, the
handicapped children we seek to help must be the first consideration.

REFERENCES

1. Private special educational effort brings into consideration complex
   issues as it relates to government and laws. For this reason, it is not
   considered in the brief treatment of history and legislation which follows. This, by no means, remarks on its importance; the student of
   special education's history is well aware of the contributions of private
   educators such as Strauss.
2. CHARLES J. HORN, JR. and NORMAN E. BOWERS, Federal Involvement
   in the Education of Exceptional Children, Institute for Research on
   Exceptional Children, University of Illinois, 1968. This is a recent and
   comprehensive review of federal legislation favoring handicapped
   children.

7

A LOOK AHEAD

IN THE PRECEDING CHAPTERS we have considered some of the
historical and present day problems associated with the field of
learning disabilities: terminology and definition, assessment, educational technology, professional training, research, parent movements, and legislation. In this chapter an attempt will be made to
sense future trends in the field of learning disabilities. Some trends
are already apparent.

1. There is a determination to clarify definition. In their first
annual report, the National Advisory Committee on Handicapped
Children determined that:[1]

> A learning disability refers to one or more significant deficits in
> essential learning processes requiring special educational techniques
> for its remediation.
> Children with learning disability generally demonstrate a dis-
> crepancy between expected and actual achievement in one or more
> areas, such as spoken, read, or written language, mathematics, and
> spatial orientation.
> The learning disability referred to is not primarily the result of
> sensory, motor, intellectual, or emotional handicap, or lack of oppor-
> tunity to learn.
> Deficits are to be defined in terms of accepted diagnostic pro-
> cedures in education and psychology.

Essential learning processes are those currently referred to in behavioral science as perception, integration, and expression, either verbal or nonverbal.

Special education techniques for remediation require educational planning based on the diagnostic procedures and findings.[2]

The reader will note the stress upon the psychological and educational aspects of learning disabilities given in these statements.

2. The use of behavioral modification techniques in remediation and assessment will probably increase. These techniques have shown promise in other fields of special education and their application to children with learning disabilities is inevitable. The full extent of their usefulness will not be known for some time. Meanwhile, the classical psychometric techniques will continue. Already, attempts are being made to computerize these procedures.

3. Technological advances in special education instructional materials can be forecast with high probability and are, in fact, underway. The entrance of large corporations into the educational materials field and the development of the Special Education Instructional Materials Center/Regional Media Center Network suggest strongly that considerable development and evaluation of instructional materials can be expected.

4. At least for the immediate future, the role of the federal government in all aspects of special education will probably expand. Recent legislation has propelled the Office of Education into support of research and demonstration activities, professional training programs, and school programs themselves. The patent need for federal assistance, and the pressure for it, foretell more massive federal involvement in the future.

Some areas do not clearly foreshadow their direction.

1. Changes in the preparation of teachers and other special education professionals are, by no means, predictable. The wide variety of educational programs now being utilized in educating the child with learning disabilities suggests the variance in present teacher training programs. Many factors will affect the direction of changes in teacher preparation programs including professional consensus, research findings, state regulations, federal assistance, and the willingness and ability of teacher preparation institutions themselves to change.

2. The role of parent organizations in special education is not clearly predictable. Having largely achieved their initial aims of local, state and federal support in education, these groups might turn

increasingly to vocational problems or educational research that will lead to the enhancement of their children's education. What is highly probable, however, is that these groups will continue to be a strong force in the shaping of special education.

3. The impact of research in the field of learning disabilities is difficult to predict. It is not so much a question of whether research can be a viable force for improvement but whether universities are willing and able to prepare researchers for work directly in schools and whether the schools are willing and able to employ researchers. It is not so much a question of whether research can answer our questions but whether we will efficiently employ research techniques currently available in the task of solving professional problems in education. It is not so much a matter of whether thousands of children are available for massive rapid coordinated research efforts, but whether schools are willing to undertake such activities and whether teachers' colleges and universities are willing to prepare their teachers in the elements of research.

Of course, problems in the field of learning disabilities must be viewed in the broad context of education generally. It is unlikely that the future of professionals associated with the education of children with learning disabilities will be unaffected by changes in the general character of education in America.

REFERENCES

1. National Advisory Committee on Handicapped Children, *Special Education for Handicapped Children,* First Annual Report (Washington, D.C.: Dept. of Health, Education, and Welfare, Office of Education, Jan. 31, 1968) p. 34.

2. A proposed federal bill (H.R. 514 and S 2218), which would provide funds for professional training, research and demonstration activities for children with "specific learning disabilities," defines such children as "children who have a disorder in one or more of the basic psychological processes involved in understanding or in using language, spoken or written, which disorder may manifest itself in imperfect ability to listen, think, speak, read, write, spell, or do mathematical calculations. Such disorders include such conditions as perceptual handicaps, brain injury, minimal brain dysfunction, dyslexia, and developmental aphasia, but such [a] term does not include children who have learning problems which are primarily the result of visual, hearing, or motor handicaps, or mental retardation, of emotional disturbance, or of environmental disadvantage."

BIBLIOGRAPHY

TESTS

AUDITORY DISCRIMINATION TEST (1958)
    Joseph M. Wepman
    Ages 5-8

    Language Research Associates
    950 East 59th St., Box 95
    Chicago, Ill. 60637

BENDER VISUAL-MOTOR GESTALT TEST FOR CHILDREN (1962)
    Aileen Clawson
    Ages 7-11

    Western Psychological Services
    Box 775
    Beverly Hills, Cal.

BENTON VISUAL RETENTION TEST (1955)
    Arthur L. Benton
    Ages 8 and over

    Psychological Corporation
    304 East 45th St.
    New York, N.Y.

CALIFORNIA TEST OF PERSONALITY (1953)
    Louis Thorpe, Willis Clark, and Ernest Tiegs
    Ages Kdg.-3; 4-8; 7-10; 9-16; adults

    California Test Bureau
    Del Monte Research Park
    Monterey, Cal.

CHILDRENS APPERCEPTION TEST (1961)
   Leopold Bellak and Sonya Sorel Bellak
   Ages 3-10

   C. P. S., Inc.
   P. O. Box 83
   Larchmont, N.Y.

DURRELL ANALYSIS OF READING DIFFICULTY (1945)
   Donald D. Durrell
   Grades 1-6

   Harcourt, Brace and World, Inc.
   757 Third Ave.
   New York, N.Y.

ILLINOIS TEST OF PSYCHOLINGUISTIC ABILITIES,
Experimental Edition (1961)
   James J. McCarthy and Samuel A. Kirk
   Ages 2-6 to 9

   University of Illinois Press
   Urbana, Illinois

ILLINOIS TEST OF PSYCHOLINGUISTIC ABILITIES,
Revised Edition (1968)
   Samuel A. Kirk, James J. McCarthy and Winifred D. Kirk
   Ages 2-6 to 10

   University of Illinois Press
   Urbana, Illinois

LINCOLN-OSERETSKY MOTOR DEVELOPMENT SCALE (1956)
   William Sloan
   Ages 6-14

   C. H. Stoelting Co.
   424 No. Homan Ave.
   Chicago, Ill. 60624

MARIANNE FROSTIG DEVELOPMENTAL TEST OF VISUAL
PERCEPTION (1964)
   Marianne Frostig in collaboration with D. Welty Lefever, John R. B.
   Whittlesey, and Phyllis Maslow
   Ages 3-8

   Consulting Psychologists Press
   557 College Ave.
   Palo Alto, Cal.

MEMORY-FOR-DESIGNS TEST (1960)
    Frances K. Graham and Barbara S. Kendall
    Ages 8.5 and over

    Psychological Test Specialists
    Box 1441
    Missoula, Mont.

PARSONS LANGUAGE SAMPLE (1963)
    J. E. Spradlin
    Journal of Speech and Hearing Disorders
    Monograph Supplement, 1963, 10, 8-31.

PEABODY PICTURE VOCABULARY TEST (1959)
    Lloyd M. Dunn
    Ages 2.5-18

    American Guidance Service, Inc.
    Circle Pines, Minn.

READING APTITUDE TESTS (1935)
    Marion Monroe
    Ages Kdg.-1st grade

    Houghton Mifflin Co.
    2 Park St.
    Boston, Mass.

SPACHE BINOCULAR READING TEST (1955)
    George D. Spache
    Nonreaders and grade 1; grades 1.5-2; grades 3 and over

    Keystone View Co.
    Meadville, Pa.

STANFORD-BINET INTELLIGENCE SCALE (1960)
    Revised IQ tables by Samuel R. Pinneau, Lewis M. Terman, and
    Maud A. Merrill
    Ages 2 and over

    Houghton Mifflin Co.
    2 Park St.
    Boston, Mass.

SYRACUSE VISUAL FIGURE BACKGROUND TEST (1957)
    Described in Wm. Cruickshank, H. V. Bice, and N. E. Wallen, *Per-ception and Cerebral Palsy.* Syrcause, N.Y.: Syracuse University
    Press, 1957.

VINELAND SOCIAL MATURITY SCALE (1953)
Edgar A. Doll
Ages birth to maturity

Educational Test Bureau
720 Washington Ave., S.E.
Minneapolis, Minn. 55414

WECHSLER INTELLIGENCE SCALE FOR CHILDREN (1949)
David Wechsler
Ages 5-15

Psychological Corporation
304 East 45th St.
New York, N.Y. 10017

WECHSLER PRESCHOOL AND PRIMARY SCALE OF
INTELLIGENCE (1967)
David Wechsler
Ages 4-0 to 6-6

Psychological Corporation
304 East 45th St.
New York, N.Y. 10017

WIDE RANGE ACHIEVEMENT TEST (1946)
Joseph Jastak and Sidney Bijou
Ages 5 and over

Psychological Corporation
304 East 45th St.
New York, N.Y. 10017

REFERENCES

BARNETT, CHARLES D., NORMAN R. ELLIS and MARGARET PRYER, "Learning in Familial and Brain-Injured Defectives." *American Journal of Mental Deficiency*, 64 (March, 1960): 894.

BARSCH, RAYMOND H., *A Movigenic Curriculum*. Madison, Wis.: Bureau for Handicapped Children, 1965.

BATEMAN, BARBARA D., "Reading and Psycholinguistic Process of Partially Seeing Children." In *Selected Studies on the Illinois Test of Psycholinguistic Abilities*. Urbana, Ill.: University of Illinois Press, 1963.

————, "Learning Disabilities—Yesterday, Today, and Tomorrow." *Exceptional Children*, 31 (Dec., 1964): 167.

————, "An Educator's View of a Diagnostic Approach to Learning Disorders." In *Learning Disorders*, vol. 1, Jerome Hellmuth, ed. Seattle, Wash.: Special Child Publications of the Seattle Seguin School, Inc., 1965.

————, "Learning Disorders." In *Review of Educational Research*, Chap. V. 36 (Feb., 1966).

BIRCH, HERBERT G., ed., *Brain Damage in Children*. Baltimore: Williams and Wilkins Co., 1964.

BRYANT, N. DALE, "Characteristics of Dyslexia and the Remedial Implication." *Exceptional Children*, 31 (Dec., 1964): 195.

BUROS, O. K., ed., *The Sixth Mental Measurement Yearbook*. Highland Park, N.J.: The Gryphon Press, 1965.

CAPOBIANCO, R. F., "Diagnostic Methods Used With Learning Disabilities Cases." *Exceptional Children*, 31 (Dec., 1964): 187

————, "Ocular-Manual Laterality and Reading Achievement in Children with Special Learning Disabilities." *American Educational Research Journal*, 4 (March, 1967): 133.

CHALFANT, JAMES C. and CORRINE E. KASS, "Training Specialists for Children with Learning Disabilities." In *Learning Disorders*, vol. 3, Jerome Hellmuth, ed. Seattle, Wash.: Special Child Publications of the Seattle Seguin School, Inc., 1968.

CLARK, ANN D. and CHARLOTTE J. RICHARDS, "Learning Disabilities: A National Survey of Existing Public School Programs." *Journal of Special Education*, 2 (Winter, 1968): 223.

CLEMENTS, SAM D., "Learning Disabilities—Who?" Abstract published in *Special Education: Strategies for Educational Progress*. (Selected Convention papers, 44th Annual CEC Convention, April, 1966a) p. 188. Washington, D.C.: The Council for Exceptional Children.

————, *Minimal Brain Dysfunction in Children*. NINDB Monograph No. 3, Public Health Service Bulletin No. 1415. Washington, D.C.: U.S. Dept. of Health, Education, and Welfare, 1966b.

Continental Press Materials. Elizabethtown, Pa.: The Continental Press, Inc. 1958.

CRUICKSHANK, WM. M. and G. ORVILLE JOHNSON, ed., *Education of Exceptional Children and Youth*. Englewood Cliffs, N.J.: Prentice-Hall, Inc. 1958.

CRUICKSHANK, WM. M. and others, *A Teaching Method for Brain-Injured and Hyperactive Children*. Syracuse, N.Y.: Syracuse University Press, 1961.

CRUSE, DANIEL B., "Effects of Distraction Upon the Performance of Brain-Injured and Familial Retarded Children," *American Journal of Mental Deficiency*, 66 (July, 1961): 86.

DELACATO, CARL H., *The Treatment and Prevention of Reading Problems*. Springfield, Ill.: Charles C Thomas, 1959.

————, *The Diagnosis and Treatment of Speech and Reading Problems.* Springfield, Ill.: Charles C Thomas, 1963.

Downing, John, *Initial Teaching Alphabet.* New York: Macmillan Co., 1965.

Dunn, Lloyd and James O. Smith, *Peabody Language Development Kits.* Circle Pines, Minn.: American Guidance Services, Inc., 1966.

Edgington, Ruth and Sam D. Clements, *Indexed Bibliography on the Educational Management of Children with Learning Disabilities.* Chicago: Argus Communications, 1967.

Fernald, Grace M., *Remedial Techniques in Basic School Subjects.* New York: McGraw-Hill Book Co., 1943.

Fitzhugh, Kathleen B. and Loren Fitzhugh, *The Fitzhugh Plus Program.* Galien, Mich.: Allied Education Council, 1966.

Frostig, Marianne and David Horne, *The Frostig Program for the Development of Visual Perception.* Chicago: Follett Pub. Co., 1964.

Getman, G. N., "The Visuomotor Complex in the Acquisition of Learning Skills." In *Learning Disorders,* vol. 1, Jerome Hellmuth, ed. Seattle, Wash.: Special Child Publications of the Seattle Seguin School, Inc., 1965.

Getman, G. N., Elmer R. Kane, Marvin R. Halgren, and Gordon W. McKee, *The Physiology of Readiness.* Minneapolis, Minn.: P.A.S.S., Inc., 1964.

Gillingham, Anna and Bessie Stillman, *Remedial Training for Children with Specific Disability in Reading, Spelling, and Penmanship.* Cambridge, Mass.: Educators Publishing Service, 1960.

Goldstein, Kurt, *Aftereffects of Brain-Injuries in War.* New York: Grune and Stratton, 1942.

Gruenberg, Ernest M., "Some Epidemiological Aspects of Congenital Brain Damage." In *Brain Damage in Children,* Herbert G. Birch, ed., p. 118. Baltimore: Williams and Wilkins, Co., 1964.

Haeussermann, Else, *Developmental Potential of Preschool Children.* New York: Grune and Stratton, 1958.

Haring, Norris and E. Lakin Phillips, *Educating Emotionally Disturbed Children.* New York: McGraw-Hill Book Co., 1962.

Haring, Norris G. and Robert W. Ridgeway, "Early Identification of Children with Learning Disabilities." *Exceptional Children,* 33 (Feb., 1967): 387.

Harmon, Darell Boyd, "Body Restrained Performance as a Contributing Cause of Visual Problems." Paper presented to Southwest Congress of Optometry, Fort Worth, Tex., 1965.

Hawkins, William F. and Alfred A. Baumeister, "The Interaction of Brain Damage and Interpolated Learning Upon Brightness Discrimination," *American Journal of Mental Deficiency,* 69 (July, 1964): 86.

deHirsch, Katrina, "Plasticity and Language Disabilities." In *Learning Disorders*, vol. 1, Jerome Hellmuth, ed., Seattle, Wash.: Special Child Publications of the Seattle Seguin School, Inc., 1965.

deHirsch, Katrina, Jeannette J. Jansky, and William S. Langford, "The Prediction of Reading, Spelling, and Writing Disabilities in Children: A Preliminary Study." Final report to the Health Research Council of the City of New York. New York: Columbia University (Contract U-1270), 1965.

Horn, Charles J., Jr. and Norman E. Bowers, *Federal Involvement in the Education of Handicapped Children*. Institute for Research on Exceptional Children, University of Illinois, 1968.

Johnson, Doris J. and Helmer R. Myklebust, *Learning Disabilities*. New York: Grune and Startton, 1967.

Kass, Corrine E., "Some Psychological Correlates of Severe Reading Disability (Dyslexia)." In *Selected Studies on the Illinois Test of Psycholinguistic Abilities*. Urbana, Ill.: University of Illinois Press, 1963.

Kephart, Newell C., *The Slow Learner in the Classroom*. Columbus, Ohio: Charles E. Merrill Books, Inc., 1960.

Kephart, Newell C., and Alfred A. Strauss, "A Clinical Factor Influencing Variations in I.Q.," *American Journal of Orthopsychiatry*, 10 (April, 1940): 343.

Kershner, John R., "Doman-Delacato's Theory on Neurological Organization Applied with Retarded Children," *Exceptional Children*, 34 (Feb., 1968): 441.

Kershner, K., R. Dusewize, and J. Kershner, "The KDK Adaptation of the Vineland Oseretsky Motor Development Tests." In J. Kershner, "An Investigation of the Doman-Delacato Theory of Neuropsychology as It Applies to Trainable Mentally Retarded Children in Public Schools." Unpublished Master's thesis, Bucknell University, Appendix B, 1967.

Kirk, Samuel A., *Educating Exceptional Children*. Boston: Houghton Mifflin Co., 1962.

————, *Diagnosis and Remediation of Psycholinguistic Abilities*. Urbana, Ill.: University of Illinois Press, 1966.

————, "The Illinois Test of Psycholinguistic Abilities: Its Origin and Implications." In *Learning Disorders*, vol. 3, Jerome Hellmuth, ed. Seattle, Wash.: Special Child Publications of the Seattle Seguin School, Inc., 1968.

Kirk, Samuel A. and Barbara Bateman, "Diagnosis and Remediation of Learning Disabilities," *Exceptional Children*, 29 (Oct., 1962): 73.

LEVINE, MURRAY, GEORGE SPIVACK and DODGE FERNALD, "Discrimination in Diffuse Brain Damage," *American Journal of Mental Deficiency,* 67 (Sept., 1962): 287.

LOVITT, THOMAS C., "Assessment of Children with Learning Disabilities," *Exceptional Children,* 34 (Dec., 1967): 233.

MASLOW, PHYLLIS, MARIANNE FROSTIG, D. WELTY LEFEVER, and JOHN R. B. WHITTLESEY, "The Marianne Frostig Developmental Test of Visual Perception, 1963 Standardization," *Perceptual and Motor Skills,* Monograph Supplement 2-V19, 1964.

McCARTHY, JAMES J., "The Importance of Linguistic Ability in the Mentally Retarded," *Mental Retardation,* 2 (April, 1964): 90.

McCORMICK, CLARENCE C., JANICE N. SCHNOBRICK and S. WILLARD FOOTLIK, "The Effect of Perceptual Motor Training in Reading Achievement." Mimeographed paper, Reading Research Foundation, Chicago, Ill., 1966.

McLEOD, J., "Dyslexia in Young Children and a Factorial Study, with Special Reference to the Illinois Test of Psycholinguistic Abilities." Mimeographed paper, University of Illinois, Urbana, 1967.

MONROE, MARION, *Children Who Cannot Read.* Chicago, University of Chicago Press, 1932.

MYERS, PATRICIA, "A Comparison of Language Disabilities of Young Spastic and Athetoid Children." Unpublished doctoral dissertation, University of Texas, 1963.

MYKLEBUST, HELMER R., *Auditory Disorders in Children.* New York: Grune and Statton, 1954.

———, "Learning Disorders—Psychoneurological Disturbances in Childhood," *Rehabilitation Literature,* 25 (Dec., 1964): 354.

———, *Development and Disorders of Written Language.* New York: Grune and Stratton, 1965.

National Advisory Committee on Handicapped Children, *Special Education for Handicapped Children,* First Annual Report. Washington, D.C.: U.S. Dept. of Health, Education, and Welfare, Office of Education, Jan. 31, 1968.

OLSON, JAMES L., "Deaf and Sensory Aphasic Children," *Exceptional Children,* 27 (April, 1961): 422.

ORTON, SAMUEL TORREY, *Reading, Writing and Speech Problems in Children.* New York: W. W. Norton and Co., Inc., 1937.

OSGOOD, CHARLES E., *Method and Theory in Experimental Psychology.* New York: Oxford University Press, 1953.

OTTO, WAYNE and RICHARD McMENEMY, *Corrective and Remedial Teaching.* Boston: Houghton Mifflin Co., 1966.

PAINE, RICHMOND S., "Organic Neurological Factors Relating to Learning Disorders." In *Learning Disorders*, vol. 1, Jerome Hellmuth, ed. Seattle, Wash.: Special Child Publications of the Seattle Seguin School, Inc., 1965.

PAINTER, GENEVIEVE B., "The Effect of a Rhythmic and Sensory-Motor Activity Program on Perceptual-Motor-Spatial Abilities of Kindergarten Children," *Exceptional Children*, 33 (Oct., 1966): 113.

PENN, JULIA M., "Reading Disability: A Neurological Deficit?" *Exceptional Children*, 33 (Dec., 1966): 243.

RAGLAND, G. G., "The Performance of Educable Mentally Handicapped Students of Differing Reading Ability on the ITPA." Unpublished doctoral dissertation, University of Virginia, 1964.

REICHSTEIN, JEROME, "Auditory Threshold Consistency: A Basic Characteristic for Differential Diagnosis of Children with Communication Disorders." Unpublished doctoral dissertation, Teachers' College, Columbia University, 1963.

ROBBINS, MELVYN P., "A Study of the Validity of Delacato's Theory of Neurological Organization," *Exceptional Children*, 32 (April, 1966): 517.

ROST, KIM J., "Academic Achievement of Brain-Injured and Hyperactive Children in Isolation," *Exceptional Children*, 34 (Oct., 1967): 125.

SCHERER, ISIDOR W., "The Prediction of Academic Achievement in Brain-Injured Children," *Exceptional Children*, 28 (Oct., 1961): 103.

SCHRANGER, JULES, JANET LINDY, SAUL HARRISON, JOHN McDERMOTT and ELIZABETH KILLINS, "The Hyperkinetic Child: Some Consensually Validated Behavioral Correlates," *Exceptional Children*, 32 (May, 1966): 635.

SCHULMAN, JEROME L., JOSEPH C. KASPAR and FRANCIS M. THRONE, *Brain Damage and Behavior*. Springfield, Ill.: Charles C Thomas, 1965.

STRAUSS, ALFRED A., "Ways of Thinking in Brain-Crippled Deficient Children," *American Journal of Psychiatry*, 100 (March, 1944): 639.

STRAUSS, ALFRED A. and NEWELL C. KEPHART, "Rate of Mental Growth in a Constant Environment Among Higher Grade Moron and Borderline Children." *Proceedings of the American Association on Mental Deficiency*, 44 (1939); 137.

————, "Behavior Differences in Mentally Retarded Children Measured by a New Behavior Rating Scale," *American Journal of Psychiatry*, 96 (March, 1940): 1117.

STRAUSS, ALFRED A. and LAURA LEHTINEN, *Psychopathology and Education of the Brain-Injured Child*. New York: Grune and Stratton, 1947.

STRAUSS, ALFRED A. and H. WERNER, "Experimental Analysis of the Clinical Symptom 'Perseveration' in Mentally Retarded Children," *American Journal of Mental Deficiency*, 47 (1942(a)): 185.

————, "Disorders of Conceptual Thinking in the Brain-Injured Child," *Journal of Nervous and Mental Disorders,* 96 (1942(b)): 153.

————, "Comparative Psychopathology of the Brain-Injured Child and the Traumatic Brain-Injured Adult," *American Journal of Psychiatry,* 99 (May, 1943): 835.

WERNER, H., "Development of Visuo-Motor Performance on the Marble Board Test in Mentally Retarded Children," *Journal of Genetic Psychology,* 64 (1944): 269.

————, "Perceptual Behavior of Brain-Injured, Mentally Defective Children: An Experimental Study by Means of the Rorschach Technique," *Genetic Psychology Monograph,* 31 (1945): 51.

————, "Abnormal and Subnormal Rigidity," *Journal of Abnormal Social Psychology,* 41 (1946(a)): 15.

————, "The Concept of Rigidity: A Critical Evaluation," *Psychological Review,* 53 (1946(b)): 43.

WERNER, H. and M. BOWERS, "Auditory-Motor Organization in Two Clinical Types of Mentally Deficient Children," *Journal of Genetic Psychology,* 59 (1941): 85.

WERNER, H. and ALFRED A. STRAUSS, "Types of Visuo-Motor Activity in Their Relation to Low and High Performance Ages," *Proceedings of the American Association on Mental Deficiency,* 44 (1939): 163.

————, "Causal Factors in Low Performance," *American Journal of Mental Deficiency,* 45 (1940): 213.

————, "Pathology of Figure-Background Relation in the Child," *Journal of Abnormal Social Psychology,* 36 (1941): 236.

WERNER, H. and B. D. THUMA, "A Deficiency in the Perception of Apparent Motion in Children with Brain Injury," *American Journal of Psychology,* 55 (1942(a)): 58.

————, "Critical Flicker-Frequency in Children with Brain-Injury," *American Journal of Psychology,* 55 (1942(b)): 394.

WISEMAN, DOUGLAS, "A Classroom Procedure for Identifying and Remediating Language Problems," *Mental Retardation,* 3 (April, 1965): 20.

INDEX